"When I heard of Carla Wills-Brandon's book *One Last Hug Before I Go,* I was immediately captured by its title and theme. As a chaplain who has been with dozens of people as they die many have had visions as they Whether the vision was of Jesus, or a deceased spouse, of a parent, or of another person or angel who came to comfort them and guide them to the other side, each vision gave something the soul needed. I am delighted that Carla has researched and written of this phenomenon."

—Pastor Jerry Bongard
chaplain and author, *The Near-Birth Experience*

"*One Last Hug Before I Go* is good news for modern times! Finally, an in-depth study of deathbed visions, which have been with us since the dawn of time, affirming when we leave this life we continue on, escorted to the heavenly realms."

—Judy Guggenheim
coauthor, *Hello from Heaven!*

"The phenomenon of deathbed visions is as old as humankind, and such visitations of angels, light beings, previously deceased personalities and holy figures manifesting to those about to cross over to the Other Side have been recorded throughout all of human history. How marvelous it is that Carla Wills-Brandon has meticulously researched the subject and presented us with an inspirational book that is certain to offer comfort, not only to the dying but to those who love them."

—Brad Steiger
Shadow World

ONE LAST HUG BEFORE I GO

ONE LAST HUG BEFORE I GO

The Mystery and Meaning of Deathbed Visions

Carla Wills-Brandon, Ph.D.

Health Communications, Inc.
Deerfield Beach, Florida
www.hci-online.com

Library of Congress Cataloging-in-Publication Data

Wills-Brandon, Carla
    One last hug before I go : the mystery and meaning of deathbed visions / Carla Wills-Brandon.
      p.   cm.
    Includes bibliographical references.
    ISBN 1-55874-779-6 (trade paper)
    I. Deathbed hallucinations. I. Title.

BF1063.D4 W55 2000
133.9—dc21

                                            00-039541

Publisher: Health Communications, Inc.
             3201 S.W. 15th Street
             Deerfield Beach, FL 33442-8190

Cover design by Andrea Perrine Brower
Inside book design by Dawn Grove

This book is loving dedicated to the three men in my life,
Michael, my husband and my two sons,
Aaron and Joshua;
along with those loved ones on the other side:
my mother, Carol Lynn Wills;
my grandmother, Bertha Wills
and
my father-in-law, Dr. Sylvan "Da" Brandon

A Gentle Journey to the Afterlife

Against the cheek,
like a cool and anointing mosslike balm;
in Velvet darkness transported.
beyond an old
and unwelcome friend,
such as "fear."
Into Light and a pleasant cacophony
of joyousness and freedom.
And no corners, nor shadows, shall invade.

James R. Wilkinson (2000)

Contents

Foreword

Though all will pass through the ingress alone, Carla Wills-Brandon has opened the approach to that entryway for all of us to view. Deathbed visions (DBVs) are ancient and similar over the centuries and in every culture. Some visions are experienced before the relative or friend dies, while other similar visions occur after death. Some visions are experienced by the dying and some by those whom they leave behind. More importantly, in most cases the DBV brings comfort to the person encountering it.

Historically—and even more so in recent history—the event of dying has been kept in hushed tones and only spoken of through funeral rights. Yet, at the same time, many occurrences surrounding death are rarely mentioned. Sometimes people present at the deathbed have seen or heard *something* leaving the body at the time of passing.

Or, the dying individual has had visions of the other side and reported them to those people at hand. Perhaps most interesting are experiences shared by the dying and those in their presence. That is, at the time of death, the dying and the people around them perceive the same, other-worldly phenomenon.

The author's quest to collect these experiences has brought within the reach of the reader a treasure rarely shared. Moreover, her insightful elucidations serve to encourage the reader to seek out such stories in their own lives. In this way, her groundbreaking work opens the possibility for much new—and necessary—understanding.

The greatest contribution of Dr. Wills-Brandon's work is in bringing to our attention the gift of comfort these occurrences offer to the people involved. What's more, her writing makes it possible for the reader to share in this comfort, and perhaps lighten the load of something that has happened in their own lives. As she so adeptly explains, these stories—in their numbers and the consistency of their details—go far beyond simple reports and as a result have far-reaching implications. Her evidentiary validation serves as a significant statement of permission for those who experience these phenomena to be open to them and to share them publicly.

Humans commonly want permission to enter into new and uncharted areas. Where such permission is not available, investigation is often stifled. Perhaps the scarcity of communal knowledge of these stories stems from a lack of that permission. Unfortunately, the religious institutions into whose context such stories are usually placed have not sanctioned such exposure. Only in those cultures where such stories are a part of the fabric of the people are they well known, where the benefits can be enjoyed by all. Western culture has not traditionally been such a community, at least thus far.

I believe people—both the dying and the mourners—are blessed by deathbed visions. These visions provide understanding, empathy, lessening of fear and obviously comfort. Consequently, these stories need to be disseminated and passed on. They can readily provide a form of solace that no religious tenet assuages.

For several decades, Dr. Carla Wills-Brandon has addressed her insightful writings to the cutting edge of the human spirit. In each of her books, she has brought to the reader's consideration new insights and creative understanding. Her works have encouraged us to go beyond the limitations we normally feel. This latest work is not an exception. *One Last Hug Before I Go* ideally will foster ongoing research and publications. Moreover, the stories included here offer to the readers rich benefits that are otherwise hard to locate. Carla is to be greatly applauded.

—Rabbi Jimmy Kessler

Acknowledgments

Putting together a book like this is a journey. Along this particular journey, I have crossed paths with many delightful people. My adventure with this work began in 1999 with Dr. Paul Bernstein. At that time, Dr. Bernstein was a member of the board of directors for The International Association for Near-Death Studies. During January of that year, the board was meeting in Houston, Texas, so I invited Dr. Bernstein to come and stay with me and my family on Galveston Island. After his meetings, he and I would sit in the backyard and talk about after-death research. When I shared my interest in deathbed visions, he suggested I contact a literary agent named John White. I soon discovered Mr. White had been involved with one of the initial deathbed-vision research ventures. I also came to find out that Mr. White was an accomplished author, with one of his books being entirely devoted to society's perceptions of death. To have an agent who was so well-versed in this particular area of study was a true godsend. Thank you, dear friend.

While retreating in the Colorado Rockies, I put together the first two chapters of this book. After doing so, I had a strong urge to ring up Christine Belleris to tell her what I was up to. Immediately, she was interested. The polish of this work is due to Christine's amazing wisdom and suggestions. She is a delight to work with.

Christine approached Peter Vegso with my idea while I was still in Colorado. Having experienced the "Vegso Genius," I knew this project needed his direction. Today, I am grateful he was willing to take one more risk with me. Thanks to Teri Peluso's persistence, the papers were drawn up and I was able to start the project.

Once the book was finished, I needed a bit more help. I am totally computer-challenged but am blessed to live across the street from two computer wizards. Dr. Keith Bly and his beautiful wife Amy often saw me running across the street—barefoot and in hysterics—over some glitch. I will forever be grateful for their patience and guidance.

Two other dear friends also contributed to the makeup of this book. Though my husband, Michael, is responsible for the photograph gracing the back of this book, our dear friend Dr. Kevin Katz provided the technical support. Rabbi Jimmy Kessler's foreword provides some opening words of wisdom. Much love and thanks to both of these wonderful men.

My husband and boys are very accustomed to Momma writing, but this book became a family affair. Our personal stories rest within these pages. Michael was very brave to let me share with you about his spiritual adventures with his father. My son Joshua's deathbed vision was the initial inspiration for this book. Both Joshua and his brother Aaron have loved listening to the words I have written about them, and on more than one occasion they have even corrected my accounts. I am so blessed to have such a wonderful bunch of men in my life.

As this work grew in scope, I became very aware that all of my loved ones on the other side were directing my thoughts. My father-in-law, Dr. Sylvan Brandon, and my grandmother, Bertha Wills, passed over in the years before work on this book began. Their journey to the other side taught me about life and the afterlife. The experience with my mother, Carol Lynn Wills—who died when I was just sixteen—initiated my own need to explore life after death. All these family members are just a whisper away, and I feel their presence as I write.

Finally, I must acknowledge the immense bravery of those who have taken the risk to share their own deathbed visions with me. By coming out into the open and saying, "I have something to tell you," you have become instrumental in healing the wounds of a society with a death phobia. Many blessings to all of you. You are all teachers on the path of spiritual enlightenment.

Chapter 1

A Visit from a Red-Haired Stranger

"Da is going to the sky!"

Joshua Sylvan Brandon

My father-in-law was sick, and the prognosis was not good. Life had been rotating around his illness for a number of months, and I was way behind on my household chores, including grocery shopping. Living on an island off the Texas coast, pickings are slim for a vegetarian palate. Every few months, I trek to the mainland for what my children call "Momma's weird food."

After one such trip taken during a long afternoon in stagnant, ninety-degree conditions, my traveling companion—my three-year-old son, Joshua—was exhausted, hot and hungry. Too tired to nap and boosted by the return to the car's air conditioning, he began demanding a breast for comfort.

While navigating the steering wheel with one hand, I reached back and patted Josh on one of his plump little legs. I knew he was becoming very tired because he was rubbing his eyes. "Honey, Momma can't nurse you right now."

"I can't go to sleep without it, Momma. You come back here so I can have some," he cried.

Knowing I was in for a battle, I decided to try logic. "Well, honey, if I come to the backseat with you, who will drive the car?"

My young son looked at me as if I were just dumber than dirt. "Let Damus drive! He can drive!" Checking my rearview mirror to make sure I didn't have another passenger with me, I asked, "Josh, who is Damus?"

With exasperation and a yawn, Josh replied, "Damus is right here, Momma. Now let him drive the car!"

No longer in a mood to argue, I said, "Damus can't drive." *There!* I thought. *That should settle this!* It didn't.

Looking stunned, Josh replied, "How do you know?"

The next day, Josh and I were again on the go. While I was driving—enjoying the scenery and the breeze that had come up—I suddenly remembered Damus. I decided to ask Joshua a few questions about his friend. Josh was busy looking at a new dinosaur toy with huge teeth, some vicious-looking creature his father had recently bought him. I asked, "Honey, who is Damus?"

With a growl he replied, "Oh, he's just some kid from the sky. A kid with red hair."

A kid from the sky! With red hair? I silently moaned. Then I thought, *Where have I gone wrong! I'm a qualified mental-health provider! Why does my child need an imaginary friend?* The stress of his grandfather's illness had been overwhelming, but I try to give Josh lots of hugs, attention and love. He goes to the office with me and is not neglected. And he's three years old, and I'm still breast-feeding. *This is just too much!* I was beside myself with another one of my "rotten mother" panic attacks. Once I calmed down, I decided I needed to know more about this Damus character.

"Sweetie, how long has Damus been around?" I asked, keeping one eye on the rearview mirror and another on the beachfront street.

"Oh, Damus just got here a few days ago," answered my son as he attacked the backseat with his fanged creature.

"Damus just got here?" I asked. "Is he a friend of yours?"

Still growling away, Josh said, "No, Mom! He just got here! He came here for Da!" "Da" was what the boys called their very ill grandfather, who was in the hospital looking very gray around the gills.

The hair on the back of my neck stood up, and I suddenly felt very chilled and overwhelmed. I pulled the car on to the beach, turned off the engine, faced my son and asked, "Joshie, is Damus here right now?"

His green eyes were already taking in the beach. "Momma, can I go play in the water? Hey! Let's build a sand castle! Maybe we will see those jelly things on the beach!"

Once again, I asked, "Honey, is Damus here?"

"No, Mom. He isn't here right now. He only comes when he wants to!" my little boy replied with much irritation. He then started to crawl out of his supposedly childproof car seat. Obviously, Damus wasn't as important to him as was seeing if any jellyfish had floated to the shore.

After playing in the ocean and running our errands, we were off again. Once in the car, I asked Josh if Damus was back. He looked to the seat beside him, smiled and said, "Yes."

I couldn't see a thing, so I asked, "What does Damus look like, honey?"

Returning his gaze to the seat next to him, Josh answered, "Mom, he looks just like a big kid." With this, he picked up his dinosaur toy and returned to his play.

Damus was with us for the rest of November while Pop's condition continued to deteriorate. Every once in a while, Josh would announce that Damus was back and all of us— myself, my husband Michael and my older son Aaron— would turn to catch a glimpse of this elusive creature. None of us ever saw Damus, which was very confusing to Joshua.

THE BEGINNING OF THE END

On Thanksgiving Day my father-in-law was out of the hospital, and he and my mother-in-law joined us for a somewhat traditional holiday feast. Michael had cooked a turkey, upside down, and I had made a tofu pumpkin pie. In spite of our cooking, everyone had a great time. Michael and I shared family gossip with my in-laws, while the boys wrestled under the table with the dog. Pop was looking better than he had in weeks. We were all very hopeful.

The day after Thanksgiving, Pop was hit by a huge stroke that completely paralyzed him. After this, he was no longer able to eat or talk. We also were never really sure if he understood what we were saying. The kids were absolutely devastated, especially my older son, who worshipped his six-foot-tall, bigger-than-life, war-hero grandfather. Our family was camped out at the hospital at least twelve hours a day, with different members taking shifts. More relatives flew to the island as doctors and nurses poked and prodded Pop. Being in the hospital before this major stroke had been very difficult for my father-in-law. For years he was an eye surgeon, a Frenchman who was used to giving orders and being in control. To see him laying helpless in a hospital bed was heartbreaking.

December crept into our lives. It was the season of Hanukkah, a favorite time of the year for Jewish children.

With potato pancakes, singing and merrymaking, Hanukkah was a time to celebrate with friends and relatives. Sadly, the season was difficult that year. Pop was dying and we all knew it. The only question was when. My sister Lila had flown from California to be with us, and she distracted my children with her eccentric aunt shenanigans. Having her with us was a blessing. She had been a hospice nurse and knew firsthand about the dying process. Michael and I were spending more and more days at the hospital, at the same time trying to keep everything as normal as possible at home for our sons. In spite of Pop's condition, we wanted them to have their eight nights of Hanukkah. Their Da would have wanted this for them, too.

In the Time of Dying

One evening, we were hosting our annual Hanukkah dinner. The house was full of loving friends. Michael and I were bursting into tears every five minutes, while our wonderful friends took turns holding us and providing words of comfort. The stress was incredible and definitely starting to take its toll. Everybody pitched in, and we were able to make the party happen. After the Hanukkah candles were lit, the latkes devoured and the wrappings of the presents scattered across the floor, my oldest son asked, "What will happen to Da when he dies?"

Our family had always been very open about death, and both of my young sons were full of questions, as usual. Josh reminded us all that Damus would take Da to the sky, but my oldest boy wasn't quite comfortable with this idea. As a card-carrying member of the International Association for Near-Death Studies, I was able to share with my children vivid tales of people who were close to death, yet who returned to life with visions of heavenly landscapes. Because of my role as a licensed marriage and family therapist, I had worked not only with the grieving, but also the dying. With this wealth of experience, I was able to speak about the many stories I had heard from clients who had been at death's door.

Stories of encounters with angels and loved ones who had already passed on were common in my office. An acquaintance of mine, Dr. Raymond Moody, had written a number of bestselling books on this topic, a phenomena he called the near-death experience (NDE). I passed his works on to my mother-in-law and my oldest son. Then I decided to share with my family an experience I had with my own mother when she was passing.

A Good-Bye Hug

When I was sixteen, my beloved mother died a terrible death. When she was just thirty-three, she was diagnosed with breast cancer. Back then, treatment for this disease was hit-and-miss at best. By the time her thirty-eighth birthday rolled around, she was on her deathbed. At five in the morning, moments before her passing, I awoke from a deep sleep and knew intuitively that my mother was dying in the hospital. A chill ran down my spine as I arose, put on my fuzzy pink bathrobe and slippers and then went downstairs to sit by the phone. Alone in the early dawn, I could feel the sadness penetrating every cell of my being. As the sun came up over the backyard orchard of fruit trees, the tears began to slowly slide down my cheeks. My beautiful, vivacious mother was gone and I knew it. About fifteen minutes later, a dear friend of hers called our home to tell me she had died. When he shared this news with me, I quietly replied, "Yes, I already know."

At this same time, two very good family friends were also getting out of their beds and slipping into bathrobes. They too had suddenly awakened at 5:00 A.M., miles away from the hospital in separate locations. As their eyes opened, they also knew my mother was departing this world and making her way to the next. At exactly the same moment, all three of us had known and felt that my mother was leaving us to begin her journey through the veil of the unknown. Just before my mother passed, a part of her had reached out to touch all three of us. She gave us all one final good-bye hug before she had to go.

Researchers call what I had experienced a deathbed

vision. As I shared this vision with my family, their expressions turned to wonder. I was confronted with a multitude of questions about life after death. I shared that my experience with my mother's death had proved to me that something—some part of us—survives after the physical body dies. I continued to explain that a deathbed vision, or DBV, is a paranormal experience or otherworldly vision that takes place—moments, minutes, days, weeks or months before the actual death—for either the one who is passing or for that person's survivors.

After sharing this information with my loving crew, my husband pulled me aside and asked, "Do you think Damus has provided a deathbed vision for Josh?" Startled by Michael's revelation, I replied, "I don't know, but now that I think of it, you just might be on to something. Damus didn't show up until Pop was really sick, and Josh said Damus was here to take Da away."

A COLORFUL VISION

That evening, Michael decided he needed some time alone with his father. I had just put the kids to bed when Michael announced he was going to spend the night with Pop in the hospital. I had tears in my eyes as I nodded silently and gave my husband a hug. Then I packed up some freshly baked chocolate chip cookies and sent them and my husband to Pop's deathbed. The next morning, my tired husband returned home looking ragged, yet at peace. The boys were upstairs watching some new video on snakes, so Michael and I sat down in the kitchen for a private talk.

"You won't believe what happened last night," Michael said with a look of amazement in his eyes. "I feel kind of funny telling you about this," he added.

Totally confused, I asked, "Is Pop dead?"

"Oh no. It's nothing like that," he answered. "Last night, at about four in the morning, I had the weirdest experience." My husband is not one to share openly at the drop of a hat, and watching him begin his tale I knew I needed to remain quiet and listen. "It was about four in the morning," he repeated, "and I was sleeping in the big, over-stuffed chair next to Pop's bed. I awoke to see this swirl of pastel color rising from Pop's chest. He looked so peaceful as this light swirl of . . . I don't know what . . . continued to rise. He is going to die soon, isn't he?" Michael asked as the tears rolled down his cheeks.

"Yes," I replied.

Later on that day, I talked to my cousin Yvonne. Yvonne had also had a strange experience at the moment of her mother's passing. "The paramedics had arrived, but Dad and I knew they were too late. I sat there with my mother as she died and watched this gray wisp of vapor leave her body. As it disappeared, I knew Mother was gone."

After sharing Michael's experience with her, she said, "Yeah, sounds like the real deal. Call me if you need help with the kids when Uncle Sava [Pop] passes."

Angel of Death

It was Friday the thirteenth. We had decided to take a break from the hospital and round up the boys for a family-night service at our temple. We belong to a great Jewish community where the rabbi is called "Jimmy" and children are allowed to run wild through the temple halls when they need to burn off energy. Once a month, many of the families in the congregation bring food for a big family meal after services. Rabbi Jimmy is a wonderful, down-to-earth guy who loves not only telling stories with a message but also hearing about the mystical experiences of others. He has also experienced a bit of the "weird" in his role as a rabbi. I have always felt comfortable asking him questions that seem strange or unusual for normal conversation.

After we had eaten, I pulled Jimmy aside and asked him if he had ever heard the term "Damus." This was all I shared with him. He suddenly took out his pen and started writing in Aramaic and then Hebrew. After pondering over his writings for a moment, he looked up and said, "Sure, *Damus* or *Damas,* depending on the spelling, translates to 'messenger of death.' According to our tradition, the messenger of death or angel of death is a positive being who assists the dying. Where did you hear this term? It isn't that common."

I was speechless! I didn't know what to say. My young son had been receiving deathbed visions. Suddenly, I started to cry. Rabbi Jimmy found my response somewhat alarming and asked "What's up?" While blowing my nose I shared with him about our strange visitor.

His only response was "Wow!"

Time to Move On!

Earlier that day, we had moved Pop from the hospital back to his room at a local elder-care facility. Both Michael and I believed he knew his time was near. Even though he could not talk, we had always known he was adamant about not dying in a hospital. Once back in his own room, with his familiar blankets, comforter and pillows, Pop seemed to relax. Michael had put a map of the world on the wall next to his bed. When I asked him why he had done this, with tears in his eyes Michael said, "I thought after he passes and leaves his body, he could use the map to help him visit those places he so loved. You know, he just loves to travel and has never gone anywhere without at least a dozen maps." That evening, Michael had also opened his window. When I asked him about this action, he replied, "Something told me to do it. I know this sounds strange, but it was like a nagging internal thought. It drove me nuts, so I finally gave in and pushed the window wide open." Then knowingly he added, "I bet when Pop leaves, he will go through the window."

After my visit with Rabbi Jimmy, I had planned on making the nightly trip to Pop's bedside and had even hired a baby-sitter for the evening. In spite of my well-thought-out plan, I was beat. Feeling absolutely drained, I decided to put off my visit and take some much-needed quiet time for my own soul. The kids were upstairs with Laura, the baby-sitter, and Michael had left for his father's room. I was flipping through television channels, looking for something to numb my emotions. I was definitely on overload. Finally I found an old Mel Brooks movie. Stretching out on the couch, I wrapped myself in my grandmother's bright blue afghan. One of my orange tabby cats had just jumped up on the couch and was making himself a bed on my chest when the phone rang. It was Michael.

"He died in my arms, Carla. He waited until the ten o'clock news was over and then he left."

My father-in-law's room was a stone's throw away from our house, so I just replied, "I love you. I'll be there in five minutes."

Pop had been a control freak with a dark sense of humor,

and his death experience had been totally and completely his. As I moved the cat and stood up, I just had to chuckle. He had waited for Hanukkah to pass because he knew how important the holiday was for his grandsons. Just to get at us all, he had chosen Friday the thirteenth to make his exit. *Such a trickster,* I mused as I folded the afghan, preparing to leave for Pop's place. Being a lover of the evening news, he had waited until the ten o'clock broadcast was over before taking flight. For a moment, I felt his presence and sighed, "You really are something. I hope your transition to the other side was a good one." Then I burst out laughing and thought, *I bet it was quite a surprise. You sure were fooled!* Pop had always been a die-hard atheist.

Later on that evening, after the family had invaded Pop's room and our friendly mortician, David, had taken Pop's body away, I returned to my house full of sleeping children and animals. Michael was helping his mother back to bed, and I knew I needed to tell my oldest son his grandfather had finally died. As I crept into his room, I tripped over a football and then a tennis racket. After landing on his bed with a "thunk" I heard, "Mom? Is that you?" As Aaron rubbed the sleep from his eyes he asked, "What is it? Is it Da?"

Embracing him close to me I smoothed his tousled hair and said, "Yes, honey. Da left."

As the tears began to spill, my son then held on to me

tightly. He sobbed his heart out for a good thirty minutes. After he cried all he could, I told him, "I love you." After that we just sat in silence.

The next morning, my three-year-old woke me up at the crack of dawn. As he pried my eyes open with his little chubby fingers, I thought to myself, *Oh, I still have to tell Josh about Pop.* Half-awake, I pulled myself out from under the warmth of my favorite afghan and said, "Sweetie, Da died last night." With this he climbed on to my bed and snuggled close to me. "How do you feel about that?"

He replied, "Sad." Then the tears came. Eventually, Michael and Aaron wandered into the bedroom and before long, the four of us were in the bed, sharing our sorrow.

All of us grieved Pop's passing in our own way. We cried and talked about our feelings as they came up. Both Josh and Aaron had a lot of questions about death and we discussed them, time and time again, with honesty and care. Each of us participated in the funeral. When it was time to lay Pop's headstone on his grave, we took matters into our own hands. With Aaron rallying the troops to the cause, we laid the stone ourselves as a family. We dug the dirt, mixed the cement and then Michael, Aaron, Josh and I set the two-hundred-pound stone into the ground. As we did so, all of us had an overwhelming sensation that Pop was watching, laughing away and wondering what on earth had possessed us to do what we were doing. After cleaning the

dirt off the stone and ourselves, we sat around the cemetery and told stories, stories about our Da who had gone to
the sky with Damus, who never visited us again.

Chapter 2

A Quest for Answers About a Possible Afterlife

"I am not the least afraid to die."

parting words of Charles Darwin

The Search Begins

The summer after my mother's death, I found myself walking into a bookstore filled with wisps of gray smoke coming from a burning Indian sage stick. As I came through the door, a life-size statue of Buddha greeted me. After rubbing his tummy for good luck, I went in search of a book that would shed light on the feeling I experienced as my mother was passing. I asked the gum-smacking twenty-something-year-old store clerk if she had ever heard of an experience like mine. As she readjusted a long string of colorful hippie beads she replied, "No, not really," and then asked, "You weren't on drugs, were you?" After I replied, "No," she then handed me *The Tibetan Book of the Dead.*

This book, also known as the *Bardo Thodol,* was originally written by Tibetan monks to assist those following their footsteps in the death transition. These spiritual individuals spend a lifetime preparing for the moment of death. As I turned the pages of this dense, complicated work, I recognized that the *Bardo Thodol* was a kind of self-help, "how to do dying well" text. The authors provide tips on what to look out for when leaving this world, going into great discussion about celestial or angelic beings. Though this book didn't completely answer all of my questions, it was a start.

I didn't find any books specifically on deathbed visions this time around, although I did buy a copy of *The Tibetan Book of the Dead,* along with four or five other books on death, dying and grief. These works taught me a lot about the many distinct belief systems different cultures around the world have about death. Though my inquiry about my personal experience wasn't to be answered that day, I was beginning to understand that death wasn't the end.

During my twenties, I would periodically ask clergy, psychologists, doctors, friends, relatives and neighbors, "Have you ever intuitively known that someone you love was crossing over before actually being told they were dying?"

I would then quickly add, "I have and it was an incredible experience! What do you think about that?" Upon hearing my petition and personal account, most of these folks would respond by looking at me wide-eyed, as if I had lost my mind. Such dramatic reactions were often followed with comments like, "A smart woman like you? You better keep that to yourself or the men in white coats will come knocking on your door!"

Following a detailed description of my deathbed experience with my mother, one close friend asked, "Couldn't you have been hallucinating? Imagining things? Have you had your eyes checked? Maybe you have cataracts? Blurred vision? Were you on drugs? Perhaps cold medicine? Did you have a fever? Were you sick? Maybe it was just a dream. You couldn't possibly have known your mother was dead before the hospital called you." After a series of such exchanges, I quickly learned I needed to exercise caution when I shared this experience.

In spite of my secretiveness, I quietly continued to look for someone who could shed some light on my confusion about my otherworldly encounter with the afterlife. Eventually, my search paid off. I even found a few friends who were willing to tell me about their unusual experiences with their dying loved ones. The most surprising tale came from a close family friend. My mother's best friend Dee told me an extraordinary story involving my own mother.

A Message from an Angel

Dee and my mother went to junior high school and high school together. The two of them had been true bosom buddies. During their junior high school years, my mother's older brother Gerald lost his life. "Friendly fire" on a boat on the Rhine River in Germany during World War II had cut his young life short. Gerald's sudden, unnecessary death absolutely devastated my grandparents. They had worshipped my tall, dark, handsome uncle and were never the same after this loss. In their eyes, Gerald could do no wrong. As my grandmother often said, "He was the perfect son." After his tragic death, my grandmother elevated Gerald to a state of sainthood. With her brother's passing, my mother's world was turned upside down. Innocence was lost and true peace never again crossed the doorway of my mother's childhood home.

My purple-haired grandmother did all she could to distract herself from her inner suffering. She often turned the record player up as loud as it would go. The heavy operatic melodies flowing throughout the house made reflection on the tragic loss of her son an impossibility. To blot out his pain, my grandfather turned to the wine bottle. Alcohol kept him from feeling the agony he had about the death of his beloved boy. Between the blaring opera music and the wine, grief was tucked away and hidden from view. With this, my mother quickly learned that the topic of Gerald's death was taboo.

Carol was my mother's name. She was a beautiful girl who never knew it. Once my uncle's light was extinguished, my grandparents forgot about this other light that needed tending. After Gerald's death, my mother's life with her parents often felt oppressive and superficial. In her house, the sweet, carefree feelings of youth had vanished. Instead, she had to search elsewhere for relief and normality.

In Dee's large, extended family, children were allowed to be children. Life felt right when my mother was at her friend's house. She and Dee did everything together. They even married two hometown boys who were the best of friends. In my cedar chest, I have wedding pictures of not only my parents, but of Dee and her young husband, Don. Naturally, when Dee and my mother had children, all of the kids became good pals. My summer vacations were spent frolicking on the beach with Dee and her family. Years later, Dee's oldest child, Dean, and I still communicate on a regular basis. We have a lot in common and seem to be taking up where our parents left off. Like our mothers before us, he and I are the best of friends. Today, Dean and I often revisit the following tale his mother told me about my mother's death.

At one time, Dee and her husband lived right on the central California coastline. Morro Bay is located in a beautiful part of the country. In the morning, a thick misty fog covers everything, but by the afternoon the skies are blue and the breeze is cool with the rich aroma of the sea. Their house was on a cliff, overlooking not only the ocean but a large mountain that sits right off the shore. Surrounded by water, this bit of land was a favorite childhood haunt of mine. During the twilight hours, the sea fog covers all but the tip of this mountain, giving it the illusion of a distant island.

A number of years ago, Michael, the boys and I were visiting my grandparents in the Central Valley. After fulfilling our family obligations, we decided to pile into the car and make the two-hour drive to the seaside to check up on Dee and her relatives. I also wanted to take my boys to see Morro Rock.

Once on the coast, visions of my youth quickly returned. The smell of the salty Pacific sea air always takes me back to the joyful memories of my childhood on the beach. On that particular day, walking into Dee's cozy, warm house felt like a homecoming. After being greeted by Dee's two small pups, there was the usual bear hug from her husband Don. Of course Dee had prepared a huge meal and we all ate ourselves silly. After dinner, Michael, Don and the boys took off for a walk, while Dee and I took care of the dishes.

Alone at last, Dee and I began talking about our favorite topic, my mother. Though it had been close to twenty years since her death, I knew this longtime friend still missed my mother as much as I did. As Dee loaded up the dishwasher, she began reminiscing about their high school days. With tears in her eyes she said, "I sure do miss her. She had the best sense of humor! Your mom was such a hoot. She loved to joke around. We did have fun back then."

Dee dried the last crystal wine goblet and then sat down at the kitchen bar. Looking at me she said, "When your mother was dying, I felt extremely helpless. I knew she was going to die, but she wouldn't say one word to me about it. It was so sad. She couldn't even talk to me, her best friend, about what she was going through." While pouring herself a glass of cola, she continued. "You know, your grandparents refused to talk about her brother's death. I think this is why she never brought up her dying. She didn't want to upset her parents. Taking care of them till the end, that was such a shame." At this point in the conversation, I remember Dee being a bit hesitant to continue. As she ran her fingers through her thick dark hair, she took a breath and said, "Now I know this is going to sound strange, but here goes." With this I pulled up a stool, put down my dishrag and was suddenly all ears.

"I knew I needed to do something for your mother, but I just didn't know what that 'something' was. Like I said, no one was talking. You and your sisters were staying with us on the coast, and your mother was back in the Valley. We were trying to give her a rest. It was the least I could do.

She had been so sick. I remember receiving a phone call from her. I think you guys were at the beach." For a moment she was silent and then she added, "Carla, she just sounded awful. I knew it wasn't good." Dee was attempting to hold back her tears, but she wasn't having much success.

After taking a long sip of cola, she collected herself, wiped her eyes and continued. "Well, one day I found myself in a bookstore. I wanted to get your mother something, but for the life of me, I could not decide what to buy. I thought maybe I would find a cheery book to brighten her mood. As I milled around the store, I realized I didn't know what I was doing. I didn't know what type of book would be good for your mother.

"Just as I was about to turn and walk out the door, I ran straight into some guy. It was as if he had come out of nowhere." Shaking her head in disbelief about an event that happened years ago, Dee stopped to take another drink. Stirring the ice cubes with her finger, she suddenly chuckled, "Geez, he wasn't bad-looking. He had a kind of angelic look to him." After reflecting a bit, she added, "He seemed to have a real sense of peace about him. I only remember seeing his face. I don't remember his clothes or even know if he had any on. As a matter of fact, I don't remember a body. All I saw was his face."

Shaking herself from the emotion of her memory, she suddenly became very serious and said, "This man, who I did not know from Adam, pulled a book down from the shelf, handed it to me and said, 'This is what you're looking for.' Stunned, I glanced down at the book he had given me. It was *The Prophet* by Kahlil Gibran. When I looked back up, this angel person had suddenly disappeared. I didn't see him leave. It was as if he had just vanished into thin air. If he had left through the doorway, I would have seen him. But I didn't. Didn't see a thing. It was all very eerie. I didn't have a clue as to what the book was about, but shaken, I went to the cashier and bought it for your mother."

This book, a lovely work of spiritual verse, gave my mother great comfort before she passed over. Who was this man Dee saw? Was he a messenger from the afterlife who knew just what it was my mother needed to assist her in her dying process? An angel? Was he one of the celestial beings described in the *Tibetan Book of the Dead*? Dee is convinced this spirit came to her for the specific purpose of aiding her in assisting my mother in dying. Dee never spoke to him, or told him about my mother, but he was able to help her purchase a book that would bring her dying friend comfort. To this day, this story is retold every time I get together with Dee. The tale has made its way through the families and is no longer seen as something unusual. Today it is seen as a blessing.

After Dee shared her encounter with the strange messenger at the bookstore, my life changed. I finally found the courage to begin seriously searching for answers that would explain my own unusual experience with my mother's passing. As I began my search this time around, I didn't care what other people thought. It became imperative for me to begin openly asking questions about death, the afterlife, contact with the deceased and spiritual visions.

In my pursuit, I was often ridiculed and have over the years become the butt of many jokes from friends and family members. "Yeah, Carla has every known book on death. We call her 'the death queen,'" or "You really believe all of that nonsense about life after death? You are crazy!" are just a few of the digs I have endured. In spite of this and with much hindsight, I know today that this initial, determined quest for answers prepared me for my son's eventual encounter with Damus, the loving angel of death.

HISTORICAL DEATHBED VISIONS

My own earnest examination of the unknown began with looking into the history of deathbed visions. This phenomena came closest to describing the experience with my mother, and it seemed like a natural path to follow. What I found was startling and mind-shifting. My whole concept of dying, death, the afterlife and otherworldly phenomena would undergo radical change.

During my middle thirties—when I was searching

metaphysical bookstores—I periodically found a tattered book that made reference to deathbed visions. Usually these books resided in a dark, dusty corner—past the strongly scented incense from India and the stacks of colorful Tarot cards—on a bottom shelf devoted specifically to topics like after-death communication (ADC), contact with loved ones after they have died; out-of-body experiences (OBEs), having the sensation of being out of the body as a result of a meditation experience or other activities; near-death experiences (NDEs), the experience of having left the body during a near-death trauma like a car accident, heart attack or other situation that brings the experiencer close to death's door; and deathbed visions (DBVs).

Published works on visions of the dying or of those at the dying person's side were extremely rare. Still, DBV phenomena were not new. Though historical information on this topic was difficult to find, my persistence paid off. After some energetic research, I began to understand that DBVs had been with us for ages.

Religious Accounts

In Christian literature, particularly in the oral traditions gathered and recorded between 55 C.E. and 100 C.E., a particular spiritual event is discussed repeatedly. The core of this event rests on the premonition of an upcoming death and is considered one of the most famous accounts given in the New Testament: Jesus of Nazareth predicting his own impending death to his followers. He tells them he knows his time of death is near and even foretells how his apostles will respond when he is arrested by the Romans. After Jesus' crucifixion, his followers recognize that the predictions have come to pass.

This DBV is part of the foundation of a major world religion and has also made its way into modern literature. From a current literary interpretation of this period in history—*A Love Divine* by Alexandra Ripley (1996)—we read the following passage where the disciple Thomas says,

> *He (Jesus) had told us (his followers) that he would be killed and be buried, to rise on the third day. I did not believe him when he said it. . . .*

The leader of a budding new spiritual movement prophesied his own death, days before the actual event.

Jesus is not the only spiritual leader to have experienced a DBV. In the Jewish mystical writings of the *Sefer Ha-Zohar* (the *Book of Splendor*)—said to have been written by the second-century Palestinian Rabbi Shimon bar Yochai—DBVs are discussed in some detail. Kabbalism, a mystical branch of Judaism, teaches that DBVs should be expected. In Rabbi Simcha Paull Raphael's wonderful book, *Jewish Views of the Afterlife* (1996), we read a quote on DBVs from the Zohar.

Thus, the Zohar teaches that "at the time of a man's death he is allowed to see his relatives and companions from the other world" (I, 219a). Similarly, "we have learned that when a man's soul departs from him, all his relatives and companions in the other world join in and show it the place of delight . . ." (I, 219a).

In this work, Rabbi Simcha also shares DBV tales of famous Hasidic rabbis. The Hasidic branch of Judaism was founded by Rabbi Israel Baal Shem Tov in the eighteenth century. As this spiritual leader died, he was able to describe to his followers how his soul was leaving his body. When he was buried, his followers said they saw his soul head toward the heavens in the form of a blue flame. Another Hasidic DBV taken from Rabbi Simcha's research is as follows:

Hasidic literature abounds with stories describing the deathbed experiences of many Hasidic Rebbes. These stories are often very detailed and show how many Rebbes made the transition from physical plane life with a sense of equanimity and calm.

There were some Rebbes able to describe the visions they witnessed as death approached. In the hour before he died, Rabbi Shmelke of Sasov saw standing beside him his deceased father. . . .

After discovering DBVs within the literature of two prominent religious traditions, my experience did not seem at all unusual! Even more examples of the deathbed vision phenomena come from death accounts of a number of historical figures.

Abraham Lincoln's Curious Dream

We are all familiar with the assassination of Abraham Lincoln. We can't escape elementary school without hearing how the sixteenth president was gunned down at a theater by the unsavory John Wilkes Booth. Though we are aware of this famous tragedy, did you know that Lincoln had a strange dream about his death several days before he was assassinated? In *Abraham Lincoln: The Man Behind the Myths* by Stephen B. Oates (1994), this dream is reported, as it was told to Lincoln's friend, Will Hill Lamon:

> *There seemed to be a death-like stillness about me. Then I heard subdued sobs, as if a number of people were weeping. I thought I left my bed and wandered downstairs. I went from room to room . . . the same mournful sounds of distress met me as I passed along. . . . I kept on until I arrived at the East Room, which I entered. There I met with a sickening surprise. Before me was a catafalque, on which rested a corpse. . . . "Who is dead in the White House?" I demanded of one of the soldiers. "The president" was the answer. "He was killed by an assassin." Then there came a loud burst of*

grief from the crowd, which awoke me from my dream. I slept no more that night; and although it was only a dream, I have been strangely annoyed by it ever sense.

Did President Lincoln have a deathbed vision about his own assassination? Was this a warning or just a fluke?

The Revelations of Sir William Barrett

One cold day several years ago, I was in Taos, New Mexico. A white-out blizzard canceled our skiing plans for the day, so, as usual, I headed straight for a bookstore. Walking through the door, I was delighted to see the shop was full of dusty, musty-smelling books. While warming myself with the shopkeeper's minty brew, I noticed a slim, green book sitting high up on the bookshelf. Pulling it down, I read the title *Death-Bed Visions*.

Quickly thumbing through the book, I realized this short work was totally devoted to the deathbed vision experience. I became very excited. Up until that point, most of the information I had gathered on this phenomena had been found in bits and pieces in strange, esoteric works. Flipping through the first few pages of my new find, I saw the book had been written by a Sir William Barrett and was initially published in 1926. Sitting on the floor of the bookstore, I thought to myself, *Yes! I have finally hit pay dirt! A whole book on DBVs!* I removed my jacket and settled into a comfortable position.

In his early days, Barrett considered himself a man of concrete science. During his younger years, he was an assistant to the famous physicist Professor John Tyndall. Like a number of scientifically minded researchers today, Sir Barrett had been a rational realist. A rational approach to the world around him ruled his way of thinking for several years. He did not begin his illustrious career by researching strange visions of the dying or those of the survivors at the deathbed. As a matter of fact, after serving as Dr. Tyndall's assistant, Barrett had become a professor himself at the College of Science in Dublin in 1873. As Colin Wilson (1986) wrote in his introduction to the rerelease of Barrett's work on DBVs, "Barrett was dragged into belief in the 'paranormal' against his will and his better judgment." After reading this, I knew I was dealing with a real, credible source.

How did this man of science find his way into this most unusual realm of study? Sir Barrett's wife specialized in gynecology and obstetrical surgery. In 1924 Barrett's life took a drastic turn when his wife told him about a number of visions a patient of hers had experienced just before dying. These particular visions had transformed the dying woman, leaving her with a great calm and sense of peace. Barrett and his wife began investigating the visions of the dying. Here is just one of the many cases he explored in his groundbreaking book.

The Assistant Matron of the Ahtahkakoops Indian Hospital, Sandy Lake Reserve, Saskatchewan, Canada, writes to me on January 28, 1925, about a patient in the hospital, as follows:

"He was a Cree Indian lad, about twenty years of age, son of Chief Papewyn, of a neighboring Reserve. He was in the last stages of phthisis (tuberculosis) and had been brought here to be cared for till the finish. He was placed in a wigwam about one hundred yards' distance.

"At last, the supreme day arrived. It was evening and I was with him. He was lying quietly in his bed when suddenly he sat up, stretched forth his arms in a yearning gesture, while an ecstatic smile broke over his face. It was not simply a smile of pleasure, but something far beyond it. The veil was lifted, and no one who was looking on could fail to realize that it was a glorious vision that met his gaze. He then lay back in his bed, looked at me with a smile, and passed away. He had been calm and collected during the day, there was no delirium; it was an unclouded glimpse of that higher life into which he was just entering."

(Signed) R. Hutchinson
Assistant Matron

This account fascinated me because the person having the vision—the *experiencer*—was an American Indian. I remember thinking, *If these visions happened in all cultures, what did that indicate about the possibility of life after death?* I also was interested to read that Sir Barrett was intrigued by the visions survivors who were at the deathbed physically or emotionally often had when a loved one was dying. I remember thinking, *Yes! That's me!*

In chapter 1, I noted how my husband, a straitlaced, no-nonsense child psychologist, had watched a pastel-colored cloud or mist leave his father's body shortly before death. Sir Barrett's work relates numerous descriptions of such visions. Here is just one.

> *Above my wife, and connected with a cord proceeding from her forehead, over the left eye, there floated in a horizontal position a nude, white figure, apparently her "astral body." At times the suspended figure would lie perfectly quiet, at other times it would shrink in size until it was no larger than perhaps eighteen inches, but always the figure was perfect and distinct. . . . This vision, or whatever it may be called, I saw continuously during the five hours preceding the death of my wife.*

During his wife's passing, this poor husband was extremely overwhelmed with what he was witnessing. According to Barrett, a doctor who was present had this to say about him. "I knew Mr. G. well, and I had occasion to know that he never read anything in the occult line; that everything [that] was not a proven fact was incompatible with his positive mind—so much so that during his vision (of which I did not know at the time) he asked me frequently if I thought he was going to become insane. . . ."

When my husband Michael initially shared the deathbed vision he had experienced, he, too, was concerned about what he had seen. His vision of his father's spirit leaving the body definitely did not agree with his previous eye-rolling, "yeah, right" attitude toward anything out of the ordinary.

Sitting on the cold floor of that Taos bookstore, sneezing from the mounds of dust that I had disturbed on the bookshelves above me, I lost all sense of time. I thumbed through Barrett's work for the rest of the afternoon. Finally I had found written material that provided me with answers. For the first time in years I felt validated.

Hard Proof

While rereading Wilson's introduction to Barrett's work, I noted a reference had been made to a study on deathbed visions. *A study,* I thought. *Now there is something I need to read! Just what does hard science have to say about DBVs?* Thankfully I knew just where to find this information. I strongly suspected that The American Society for Psychical Research would have information on this study. The ASPR, which has been in existence since 1885, is a scientific organization dedicated to the methodical investigation of the paranormal. Being a member of this association, I decided to call the ASPR head office in New York to see if I could find the study. Once again, I was on the right track. The ASPR sent me a complete study on deathbed visions by researchers Karlis Osis and Erlandur Haraldsson.

After reading through the study, I discovered that this research had been published in a 1977 book, *At the Hour of Death*. Believe it or not, *my literary agent,* John White, edited Osis and Haraldsson's book on deathbed visions! When we began our relationship I was working on another book and was totally unaware of his connection to these two authors. (Coincidence? I think not.) With this realization, I suddenly felt as if powers greater than myself were directing my quest. As I reread the study on deathbed visions, I became convinced that not only was I being directed by unseen forces, but pushed!

Over a period of nearly two decades, Drs. Osis and Haraldsson investigated the visions of the dying, building on Barrett's work in an extraordinary way. Dr. Karlis Osis, director of research at the American Society for Psychical Research in New York City, and Dr. Erlandur Haraldsson, a professor of psychology at the University of Iceland in Reykjavik, surveyed the deathbed experiences of the dying in the United States and India. By questioning doctors and nurses who were present during the final hours of more than one thousand hospitalized patients, Osis and Haraldsson were able to gather some very interesting facts about the dying experience. Here is just a bit of what they found.

> *The main findings of the pilot survey ("Deathbed Observations by Physicians and Nurses," Osis [1961]) were confirmed in the present survey in both cultures (American and Indians from India). Again (as was found in the pilot study), four-fifths of the apparitions (visions) were "survival related"; that is, they portrayed deceased persons and religious figures. This is in sharp contrast to the hallucinations of a normal population. Three out of four apparitions were experienced as having come to take the patients away to a post-mortem modus of existence, to which 72 percent of them consisted. More patients responded with serenity, peace and elation (41 percent) than with negative emotions (29 percent) to this ostensible invitation to die.*
>
> *The data were analyzed for interactions with various medical, psychological and cultural factors which could cause or shape hallucinations. In conformity with the survival hypothesis (Death is the transition to another mode of existence), the deathbed visions were found to be relatively independent of these factors as they were assessed in the population surveyed.*

In other words, the researchers discovered that in these two different cultures, true DBVs did not appear to be caused by high fever, illness or medication. They added that sex, age, education, socioeconomic status and religious affiliation appeared to have little impact on the DBVs they investigated. Finally, they compared DBVs with the hallucinations some psychiatric patients experience.

> *The content of the dying patients' hallucinations (deathbed visions) were analyzed and found to be different from those of hallucinations in the general population and the mentally ill. For example, hallucinations of the dying are usually visual, . . . Terminal patients were reported to have seen apparitions of the deceased, rather than of the living, two or three times more often than the general population. Of all the apparitions identified (recognized persons appearing to the dying in a deathbed vision), 90 percent were (deceased) relatives of the patient; of these, 90 percent were close relatives: mother, father, spouse, sibling and offspring. This occurs infrequently in the hallucinations of the general population.*

THE COMFORT OF DBVs REVEALED

After I read through this study, I "just happened to have" a visit with a longtime acquaintance. She was very upset about her mother's recent passing. We went to a small quiet Mediterranean cafe for a bite of lunch and privacy.

As we finished our meal, she said, "You know, when Mom was dying, she said something very weird." The word "weird" quickly distracted me from my coffee.

"Oh?" I replied. My friend now had my complete attention. "What was so weird about it?" I asked.

She told me, "A few hours before Mom passed, she became clear as a bell. I mean she was her same old self again. Up until that point, she seemed confused and not really with it. I was sitting with her watching the evening news when suddenly she opened her eyes, sat up, looked directly at the ceiling and said, 'Yes, dear, I know. I will be there in a second.' After this, she laid back down, turned to me and said, 'Hello.' For a few moments we had a bit of a conversation about the kids and my husband. Then she ended our brief talk by saying, 'I love you very much.' After that, she passed."

After wiping a tear from her cheek, my friend continued. "Initially, my exchange with my mother before she died was very confusing to me. At first, I thought maybe she had been hallucinating before she spoke directly to me, but then I thought about it for a while. If she was hallucinating, why was she so clear and able to talk coherently, not only to whomever she was referring to as 'dear,' but with me? For weeks after her death, this one thought really bugged me. Several months later, I had a childhood memory. My father died when I was very young, but I do remember he was the only person my mother ever called 'dear.' You might think this is strange but, I wonder, could he have come back to help Mom die?"

My friend's sharing about her mother's passing sounded just like several of the DBVs described in Barrett's book. Yes, I thought to myself. *I'm on the right path. Not only have I received validation of my own DBV from the writings of Barrett, Osis and Haraldsson, but now from a friend. Death is not the end. Our loved ones are still alive on the other side.* With a smile, I looked at my bewildered girlfriend and replied, "Sounds like your mother had a very special visitation before she died."

Chapter 3

Afterlife–An Ancient Concept Revisited

"I still live . . . Pretty. . . ."

parting words of Daniel Webster

Belief in life after death has been present across time and cultures. Fifty thousand years ago, Neanderthal people took a great deal of time and care in burying the dead in a ritualistic manner. The skeletons were arranged and bound according to a specific method. Unless there was some belief in an afterlife, one has to wonder why people in that culture would take precious time away from finding necessary food and shelter to perform elaborate death rituals.

Ancient Egyptians buried their *Egyptian Book of the Dead* with their loved ones. This particular guide to the afterlife had specific instructions. The post-mortem manual provided for the newly departed soul information on correct behavior after death. The book was actually read to the corpse as it was prepared for burial. People in ancient Egypt believed that if the dead soul did not follow these instructions, then merging with Osiris—the god of fertility and resurrection—would be impossible. Along with this preparation, the body of the departed went through an elaborate mummification process to ensure that the spirit could have a resting place in the other world. The mummification process involved months of preparation.

At the British Museum of Natural History in London, the results of such extreme after-death treatment of the human body are on exhibit. Special good-luck charms were tied into the cloth wrapped around the mummy. Body parts were stored in specially designed jars for internment.

Phrases from the *Egyptian Book of the Dead* were often inscribed on the mummy itself. Pets, servants and spouses were also mummified to accompany the departed into the next life. Large structures and pyramids housed the mummies and were often booby-trapped to keep grave robbers from infiltrating the tombs.

Consider also the Native American culture. The following excerpt is from Walt Whitman's *Leaves of Grass* (1891). In this verse, he describes the death of a Seminole Indian chief named Osceola who died of a broken heart in a Florida prison. The Seminole in this tale takes great pains to dress for his departure. Then he says good-bye to his beloved family and moves on.

When his hour for death had come,
He slowly rais'd himself from the bed on the floor,
Drew on his war-dress, shirt, leggings, and girdled the belt
    around his waist,
Call'd for vermilion paint (his looking glass was held before
    him),
Painted half his face and neck, his wrists, and back-hands,
Put the scalp-knife carefully in his belt—then lying down,
    resting a moment,
Rose again, half sitting, smiled, gave in silence his extended
    hand to each and all,
Sank faintly low to the floor (tightly grasping the tomahawk
    handle),
Fix'd his look on wife and little children—the last. . . .

Again, consider the motivation for going through such ritualistic activity. Do a variety of cultures—ancient and more recent, including our own—anticipate deathbed visions, near-death experiences and after-death communications and try to prepare for them?

According to history, some Egyptians were required to experience near-death experiences in order to gain access into certain mystical cults. These NDEs were often induced by bringing the Egyptian initiate close to death. With this experience, the individual knew what to expect at the moment of death. Could these NDEs form the foundation for the instruction found in the *Egyptian Book of the Dead*?

Like the ancient Egyptians, the Tibetans also wrote a number of volumes to assist the dying in traveling to an afterlife. The *Tibetan Book of the Dead* is another example of an ancient guide to the death and dying experience. Many of its passages provide vibrant descriptions of not only the death process, but of the other world. The following excerpt from the *Tibetan Book of the Dead* is quite enlightening. Here we see how the departing soul is instructed on what to expect after death. Notice how detailed and intricate the description is.

O Child of noble family, when your body and mind separate, the dharmata (light being) will appear, pure and clear, yet hard to discern, luminous and brilliant, with

*terrifying brightness, shimmering like a mirage on a plain
in spring. Do not be afraid of it, do not be bewildered. This
is the natural radiance of your own dharmata, therefore
recognize it. . . . You have what is called a mental body of
unconscious tendencies, you have no physical body of flesh
and blood, so whatever sounds, colors and ray of light occur,
they cannot hurt you and you cannot die. It is enough to
recognize them as your projections. Know this to be the
bardo state.*

The ancient Greek poet Homer also composed elaborate
portrayals of the afterlife. In his great epic, the *Odyssey,* he
tells how the hero Odysseus descends into Hades, or Hell.
Homer also described another type of afterlife. Elysium,
ruled by Rhadamanthus, is where the righteous were
thought to go upon death. Here, life was beautiful and the
soul experienced perfect happiness.

Moving Forward

Just where did the above description of the afterlife from
the *Tibetan Book of the Dead* and Homer come from? I
believe these ancient writings, like the *Egyptian Book of
the Dead,* were greatly influenced by deathbed visions and
near-death experiences. Remember that some ancient cultures often induced near-death experiences to produce a
spiritual experience. John White's book, *A Practical Guide*

to Death and Dying (1988), reports that the ritual of baptism may have similar roots in the attempt to bring about an out-of-body experience (OBE):

> . . . *(A)ccording to esoteric Christianity, the true purpose of baptism is to induce an OBE and, thereby, demonstrate to the convert or initiate the reality of life after death. Baptism requires, from the esoteric point of view, that the person be held under water to the point of nearly drowning. This near-death experience, with an out-of-body experience likely to be included as part of it, initiates the person into the psychic mysteries. . . .*

Given this view of baptism, consider the following narration of life after death from a teenager living in the East St. Louis projects, who almost drowned when he was about ten years of age. Like the initiate being baptized in some ancient, esoteric faiths, he too had a near-death experience. This recent account was documented by NDE researcher Dr. Melvin Morse in his wonderful book, *Transformed by the Light* (1992).

> *When I floated out of my body . . . suddenly I realized we were all the same. There ain't no black and there ain't no white. I saw a bright light and I knew it was all the colors there were, everything was in the light.*

Notice how similar this modern NDE account is to the passage taken from the centuries-old *Tibetan Book of the*

Dead? Is this interpretation just the product of an over-active imagination or wishful thinking? I don't think so.

Descriptions of beauty appear often in modern afterlife experiences. In *Transformed by the Light,* Dr. Morse reported another deathbed vision with interesting depictions of the afterlife. An eleven-year-old boy suffered from lymphoma. His family was praying with him when suddenly he sat up and said

> *There are beautiful colors in the sky! There are beautiful colors and more beautiful colors. You could double jump up there! Double jump!*

The boy's condition worsened, but the next morning,

> *[o]pening his eyes wide, he asked his grieving parents to "let me go. Don't be afraid," he said, "I've seen God, angels and shepherds. I see the white horse." He told his family they mustn't feel sorry for him, because he had seen where he was going and it was beautiful.*

Doesn't this boy's description of the afterlife sound like a lovely fairy tale? Perhaps for that reason so many artists and authors in addition to Homer explore life after death. Travel to the other world has been played out in literature, art, poetry and other media over the centuries. Archaeology also suggests that humankind's concern with life after death has a long history. In ancient cultures, as in the

Egyptian and the American Indian, preparation for other-worldly travel often involved a great deal of planning; the body of a loved one might be buried with all of his or her most precious belongings. Archaeologists have unearthed from ancient gravesites poetry, clothing, food products, boats, jewelry and a host of otherworldly accoutrements. In Oriental cultures, even money has been found. Burial preparation was often extensive and quite complicated. If humans didn't believe in an afterlife existence, such elaborate burial rituals would seem meaningless.

Angel and Spirit Visitations

Literature offers many encounters with spirits from the other world. My favorite Christmas tale is *A Christmas Carol*. In this delightful story we learn how Ebenezer Scrooge is visited by three spirits from the other world. These spirits come to warn Scrooge that if he doesn't change his grumpy, stingy ways, drastic consequences will visit him. To learn these lessons, he sojourns with each of these ghostly creatures to different periods in his life: the past, the present and the future. Scrooge's spirit encounters alter his personality, and after the experience he is "reborn" into a loving, kind and giving man.

William Shakespeare also wrote about spirits visiting from the afterlife. Hamlet receives a visit from his deceased father. Unknown to Hamlet, there was a plot to kill him. His dead father briefly returns from the grave to warn his son. In the very beginning of this tale, Hamlet is visited by angels.

A lesser-known literary piece that concerns visitations is "The Bowmen," a short story by Arthur Machen. This tale is based on an angelic encounter that servicemen with the Allied troops experienced during the bloody battle of Mons. According to legend, in August 1914 during World War I, thousands of soldiers saw a host of angels descend from the sky to assist them in battle. Sadly, many of the soldiers perished and they lost the battle, but Machen's spiritually based short story boosted morale and the war effort.

As in *Hamlet* and "The Bowmen," angels are found throughout ancient literature and myths across numerous cultures: Greek, Hebrew, Hindu, Roman, Persian and Muslim. One of the most famous of angels, Michael the Archangel, has a special standing not only within Judaism and Christianity, but within the Muslim religion as well. Visions of celestial beings are threaded throughout the Old and New Testaments. From the Old Testament we read about Moses' most famous encounter with an angel. "And the Lord appeared unto him in a flame of fire out of the midst of a bush . . . " (Exodus). Today, when we want to infer that we have just had an incredible happening, many people say, "I had a burning-bush experience." For early

Christians, angels were not seen as winged creatures with large halos. They were seen as celestial beings who came to offer assistance to humankind.

One function of angels at the moment of death is to provide comfort and guidance to the dying. In the poem "The Guardian Angel" by Robert Browning, we read about an angel escorting the dying to heaven.

> —And suddenly my head is covered o'er
> With those wings, white above the child who prays
> Now on that tomb—and I shall feel thee guarding
> Me, out of all the world; for me, discarding
> Yon heaven thy home, that waits and opes its door.

Osis and Haraldsson's *At the Hour of Death* (1977) offers another view of an otherworldly angel visit where the angels serve as a peaceful presence to the dying.

> He was unsedated, fully conscious and had a low temperature. He was a rather religious person and believed in life after death. We expected him to die, and he probably did too as he was asking us to pray for him. In the room where he was lying, there was a staircase leading to the second floor. Suddenly he exclaimed, "See, the angels are coming down the stairs. The glass has fallen and broken." All of us in the room looked toward the staircase where the drinking glass had been placed on one of the steps. As we looked, we saw the glass break into a thousand pieces without any apparent cause. It did not fall, it simply exploded. The angels, of

course, we did not see. A happy and peaceful expression came over the patient's face and the next moment he expired. Even after his death the serene, peaceful expression remained on his face.

As we are seeing, otherworldly creatures such as angels have long been a source of fascination.

Within a number of ancient civilizations, great care was taken to appease specific spirits. Today, in certain African cultures, an age-old fear of upsetting the spirits of the deceased continues. Recently, my family and I went to Jamaica and received a taste of this long-standing concern.

Much of the culture in Jamaica is influenced by African-based spirituality, brought over during the old slave-trading days. While we were visiting the lush, tropical island of Jamaica, we took a second trip to Rose Hall, a centuries-old plantation and mansion located just outside Montego Bay. I wanted to take some photographs of several of the rooms in the mansion.

Rose Hall was once the proud property of Mrs. Anne Palmer, who apparently wasn't a very nice mistress. She is believed to have murdered not just one, but three of her husbands. Hundreds of years later, the locals living in the area make it a point of leaving the plantation grounds by six o'clock in the evening, because as I was told, "Mrs. Palmer comes out and roams around her house!" Several deaths—other than those of her husbands—have been attributed to

Mrs. Palmer, the ghost of Rose Hall. Some locals claim to have seen her spirit "floating around the grounds." After hearing this, I asked, "Do Mrs. Palmer's murdered husbands ever join her during her travels?" In response to this question, I received a wide-eyed, fearful stare!

Conventional pictures taken in the rooms where the murders occurred have provided some interesting results. In the old dungeon at the mansion, visitors have left odd photographs of various rooms. Streams of light cross several posted photographs, and in one picture a face is very visible. With the photographs we took, strange lights and very unusual shading were most apparent. A series of particularly unnerving pictures were taken in a room where one of the brutal murders occurred. In four different photographs of this room, a strange white light was seen. Michael and I both tried to find a rational explanation for this, such as angle of the photographs, light from other sources or camera problems, but we came up empty-handed. If Anne Palmer continues to visit her old stomping grounds, who is to say the dying can't be visited by deceased loved ones, spirits and angels?

Setting the House in Order

Throughout history, a messenger of death or angel of death has provided the dying with an opportunity to "tie things up" before passing. In researching the dying experience, I have found many reports before 1000 A.D. of people knowing when they were going to pass. Visions of God, angels and deceased loved ones forewarned them of their upcoming departure. This warning gave them time to say good-bye to family and friends, review their lives, resolve old grievances and ask forgiveness from those they had harmed.

In the mid-nineteenth century, Robert Browning, the English poet, had a sister-in-law who knew exactly when she was going to die. Browning's deceased wife, poet Elizabeth Barrett Browning, visited this woman in a dream. In the dream she asked Mrs. Browning when the two of them would be reunited, and Elizabeth Barrett replied, "My dear, in five years" (Flammarion [1922]). Four years and eleven months later the sister-in-law passed.

According to historical accounts, angels and the deceased not only visit the dying, but they often appear to bring a message to the living. Dante, the author and poet who lived from 1265-1321, received an extraordinary otherworldly message about the death of a woman he deeply loved, upon whom the central character for *The Divine Comedy* is based. From Flammarion we read,

> *The poet tells us that he had a kind of terrible vision of the end of the world, . . . and believed that he saw coming toward him a friend, who told him, "Your excellent lady has departed this world." An angel bore her to the skies.*

Aid and Comfort

Reports continue to this day of otherworldly creatures who travel across the threshold between life and death to bring comfort and aid. Several years ago, a friend of mine shared a story that brought tears to my eyes. Her mother-in-law had been very sick and living quite a distance from her and her son. Because the mother didn't want to upset her family, she decided to not burden them with the state of her health. Her son and daughter-in-law were grief-stricken when the mother's death occurred. My friend told me, "We felt so incredibly guilty. It devastated us to think Mother died alone and we were not there to comfort her during her final moments." Several weeks after the mother's death, my friend had a strange visit.

She was asleep next to her husband when suddenly she was awakened. Standing at the foot of her bed was her deceased mother-in-law. At first my friend thought she was dreaming, but quickly realized she was wide awake. The mother looked at her and said, "There is no reason for you to feel guilty. Tell my son I am just fine." With this, she suddenly disappeared. My distraught friend quickly awakened her sleeping husband, and passed on to him the message she had received. After they had both reclaimed their wits, this visit brought them a great sense of peace and relief.

Bill and Judy Guggenheim recently wrote a wonderful book about the after-death communication, or ADC, phenomena. This particular book, an assemblage of experiences from people who have had contact with deceased loved ones, is titled *Hello from Heaven* (1997). The work provides a great deal of anecdotal evidence about an afterlife. Their wonderful research also provided reassurance for my husband when he had an ADC with his departed father.

The night my father-in-law died in my husband's arms was a long one. After his passing, all of the family made their way to his deathbed. I went home to tell my older son his Da had passed, comforted him and then returned to Pop's residence for one last time to say good-bye. When I saw my deceased father-in-law laying in his bed, he had an extremely serene expression on his face. It was obvious he had a good passing.

For hours after that, we were sad, but also periodically joking with one another. This is just how Pop would have wanted it. The family sat around Pop's body and shared tales of his life. Between the laughter and the tears, every once in a while one of us would stroke or pat the body that had once housed the soul of our beloved Da.

The mortician who came to claim the body was a sweet guy named David. David had just lost his mother. He too was having a hard time with his recent loss. David was teary-eyed and tired, so we helped him roll Pop's remains out to the awaiting hearse. At this point, the scene turned into a dark comedy, one that most likely had my father-in-law chuckling on the other side of the veil. The wheels of the gurney kept running over my feet, it was dark outside, rain was falling, there was a serious chill in the air and, for a moment, nobody knew where the hearse was. After David drove off with the body, I remember thinking to myself, "This is so typical of this family. Even with death, it's chaos and confusion to the end." Michael and I then crawled into our own car to return to our house full of snoring children, pets and one exhausted baby-sitter. After consoling our oldest son Aaron, both of us made our way to our bed and were fast asleep as soon as our heads hit the pillow.

The following morning, I awoke early to find my husband's side of the bed had been taken over by two large cats. As they stretched, meowed, turned over and went back to sleep, Michael was nowhere to be found. The house was silent.

Making my way to the kitchen for a cup of strong coffee, I found Michael sitting at the breakfast nook. He seemed very rested and at peace. After giving him a quick kiss hello, I went to start up the coffee. Suddenly, I found him standing right in front of me. "Honey, he's all right. Pop is all right."

Looking at him strangely, I asked, "Are you feeling okay?"

Taking my arm, he led me to the couch in the sitting room. "Carla, I saw him. He was sitting right here. Right here in his usual spot."

Quickly I looked at the end of the couch and then back at my husband. "What are you talking about?" I asked.

Sitting down in Pop's old place on the green sofa, he continued. "When I got up this morning, I came down the stairs, walked through the dining room and began to make my way into this room, to go get the newspaper. That's when I saw him, and do you know what? He was healthy. He wasn't sitting in his wheelchair. Pop looked like the picture of health. He came back just to let me know he was okay."

Pop returned for one brief moment to let his favorite son know he was happy and safe. As my mother made her way to the door of death, did she stop by my bedroom to let me know she too was all right? Is death really just a change of address? And if so, can the deceased return to assist us during our hour of grief? Do our departed loved ones continue to care for us or even worry when we are in a bad way? I believe love crosses all boundaries, even death. When we need our loved ones on the other side, I am convinced they hear our pleas.

As we have seen, it appears as though angels, spirits and departed loved ones have for ages been providing reassurance for both the living and the dying. For Michael to see

Pop whole, healthy and happy was comforting. This vision softened his grief. Michael is not the only one to have been blessed with such a healing vision. Taken from Barrett's *Death-Bed Visions*, here is an example of a turn-of-the-century DBV with characteristics that are similar to Michael's vision. This particular account also provided a mourning family with hope and encouragement.

> *An old man named John George . . . lay dying. He and his wife, Mary Ann George, had a great sorrow that same year in the death of their youngest son, Tom, a young man who had been killed on the railway line on which he worked.*
>
> *The dying man had been quiet for some time as though sleeping, when he suddenly looked up, opened his eyes wide, and looking at the side of the bed opposite to where his wife was, exclaimed, "Why, Mother, there is Tom, and he is all right, no marks on him. Oh, he looks fine." Then after another silence he said, "And here's Nance too." A pause, then, "Mother, she is all right. She has been forgiven." And very soon after he passed away, taking with him a sorrow which had long pressed upon the mother's heart, for Nance had fallen into sin, and had died soon after the child was born, and as the poor mother thought, "never having had time to repent."*

Imagine the comfort felt by a dying father as a loving son comes to escort him to the other side. The son's wounds from his accident are gone. The surviving wife and mother also receives a gift from her husband's DBV. Not only is she comforted that her dead son is well, but she also learns about the fate of her daughter, Nance. She discovers from her husband's vision that, like her son, Nance, too, no longer suffers.

My Treasure to Share

Over the years, I have collected a variety of visions the dying have had before passing. Many people across the country and in different parts of the world have openly shared with me the treasured visions of their departing loved ones. After collecting so many of these accounts, I began to realize that such experiences needed to be shared with the public. As I present the deathbed visions that appear through the remainder of this book, you need to understand that, with a number of the accounts, the names involved have been changed to protect the privacy of the people and the family involved. Many families have asked that I not divulge their personal, identifying information.

Hard science continues to dismiss otherworldly encounters, believing they are the product of an overactive imagination, psychological or physical illness, medication, wishful thinking and a host of other consequences. Many people have had difficulty sharing their DBVs with others.

Ridicule, condescension and a fear of being viewed as strange keep numerous events hidden, as mine had been for so long.

My purpose in preparing this book is not to convince scientists of existence after death. By handing these accounts over to you, I hope to give you something to think about. Possibly you have heard a tale about a strange visitation from a loved one who was passing. If so, most likely you were told by health-care professionals, friends or even family that such a vision or visitation was just a hallucination.

You might be confused about the "stare" your loved ones had in their eyes before departing. When dying, a departing person may fixate on a particular area of the room. What are they staring at? A vision? Were they comforted? Could they have been catching a glimpse of what awaited them after death? In Osis and Haraldsson's work, deathbed visions often consisted of views of beautiful landscapes.

Maybe you have had an unusual experience just before a loved one passed, as did my son with Damus. If so, you may have found this experience difficult to understand or explain. Perhaps you are searching for answers. Reading the DBV accounts of others who have also witnessed or experienced the unexplainable will hopefully provide you with a sense of *Oh, I'm not the only one!* Knowing we are not alone in our otherworldly experiences can be most reassuring and spiritually uplifting.

While reading the experiences presented in the following chapters, notice how consistent DBVs tend to be with one another. Humankind's first recollection of DBVs and today's experiences exhibit a great deal of uniformity.

The current-day DBVs I have collected and deathbed accounts from other sources validate this notion of consistency. They also support the groundbreaking DBV research of Osis, Haraldsson and Barrett. Drs. Osis and Haraldsson found a great deal of concurrence in the deathbed visions of both Indian and American patients. This consistency validates afterlife visions that have been passed down from one generation to the next. As John White stated so eloquently in a recent letter to me, which referred to the consistency found in Osis and Haraldsson's research:

In both cultures, which have widely differing attitudes toward death and widely differing assumptions about postmortem experience, a surprising conclusion emerged: the experiences of the dying are essentially the same, regardless of culture and religion. The dying perceive the apparitional presence (vision) of deceased relatives, friends and loved ones, and sometimes religious and mythical figures, who come into the room where the dying person is. They come from a splendid, nonterrestrial (otherworldly) environment, characterized by light and peace, in order to greet the dying person into his or her new condition. These perceptions are veridical (genuine). [T]he research (in both cultures) ruled out all alternative explanations such as hallucination due to medication or lack of oxygen to the brain. The findings point strongly toward the continued existence of the human personality after bodily death.

As you read through the following chapters, ask yourself, "Why are these individual DBV experiences so similar across cultures, ages, races and religions? Is there some grand scheme to the dying experience? Is the common saying, 'You die alone,' just a false belief that our society continues to foster? Are we greeted at death's door by those who have loved us in the past? Might the angels and light beings, described throughout history and in every culture, be a reality?"

My desire to examine the thread of DBVs from yesterday to today is based on my hope that, some day, the prospect of death will no longer be feared. To really know that we do not die alone is a true blessing. All of us deserve this peace of mind.

As Basil Wilberforce so beautifully stated for Barrett's book many years ago: "I believe no soul is left to wing its viewless flight to Paradise in solitude. . . . I believe the chamber of the dying is filled with holy angels."

Examine the evidence for yourself. As you travel through

the incredible deathbed visions documented in this work, remember the famous words of Walt Whitman:

All goes onward and outward
Nothing collapses
And to die is different from
What anyone supposes
and luckier.

Chapter 4

Family Reunions

"Mamsha!" (Mother!)

parting words of Waslaw Nijinsky

Deathbed visions have played a very important role in both my personal and professional life. In my personal life, they have assisted my grief process. Because of my encounter with these visions, I know for certain that life goes on after death. The comfort that comes from understanding my departed loved ones are safe—alive and well on the other side—is boundless.

When someone I know passes away, I am sad that I will no longer be able to talk, hug, sit, have a meal or physically be with that person. My grief isn't related to never seeing them again. My sense of loss is more about not being able to reach out and readily "touch" my loved ones in the here and now. This change in the state of the relationship is what I most grieve.

Over the years I have learned that with death, only the method of interpersonal connecting changes. The dying appear to move on to a new existence, leaving us here to finish out our tasks in this life. In spite of these alterations, love continues to cross all boundaries. Research into this phenomena has proven this to me repeatedly. Knowing what I know about life after death, I often wonder which one of my deceased relatives will greet me at death's door. As I take my last few breaths, who will lovingly extend the hand of comfort to me? I find most exciting and reassuring the prospect of a future family reunion with long-lost loved ones.

My favorite type of deathbed visions have always involved visitation from deceased family members. Such visitations soothe both the living and the dying. They make the death transition easier for the dying and lessen the burden of grief for surviving family members. In some cases, even long-standing family disputes appear to be resolved. Consider the following account.

On May 22, 1972, the Duke of Windsor took his last breath. His abdication of the English throne and subsequent marriage to the American divorcée Wallis Simpson had given his mother, Queen Mary, a great deal of grief. According to an article by Ian Watson, in a November 1986 issue of the *Sunday Telegraph*, when dying the Duke was heard quietly saying, "Mama . . . Mama . . . Mama . . . Mama" just before he died. Do you think Queen Mary came to escort her son, who had caused her such pain during her time on earth, to the afterlife?

REACTIONS

People who are close to death commonly call out the name of a dead relative. To finally reunite with loved ones who have passed on must be a wonderful feeling. Centuries ago, as a man or woman lay dying—surrounded by loved ones, with a favorite pet at the foot of the bed—seeing deceased relatives was viewed as a normal affair. Those at the deathbed would often ask, "Who do you see? How are they? Do they have a message for me?" Today, such events continue to occur, but are we listening? Are we open to the lessons of the dying?

With deaths taking place more often than not in hospitals and nursing homes, DBVs are often dismissed. Periodically, a kind nurse or doctor does take note and offer support. In reading the following DBVs, notice how comforted the dying person is at seeing a familiar face from the other side. Jenny Randles and Peter Hough offer us the following account from their book, *The Afterlife* (1993).

Sheila Mendoza is a charge nurse who works in the intensive care unit wards of a large hospital in Texas. She has watched many people die and admits that she had become rather hardened to the process. However, nothing prepared her for one night in 1982 when the most remarkable event that she had ever witnessed was to take place.

Sheila was on night shift, paying special attention to a man who had been in the hospital for some days. Although under close care, he was not thought to be in any danger nor seriously ill.

At about 8 P.M. he began talking very lucidly about a loved one whom he longed to see. Sheila could not tell who this person was, but it was obvious that the man had not seen her in many years and never expected to do so again. The impression is that she must have passed away some years before. The man then slipped from his mumbling into a restless sleep.

At about 9:30 he began talking about this person again, and his vital signs also began to fall. Fearing the worst, more medical staff was brought in, but the man slid into a comatose state.

Then the patient became wonderfully alert, as some people do very near the end. He looked to one side, staring into vacant space. As time went by, it was clear he could see someone there whom nobody else in the room could see. Suddenly, his face lit up like a beacon. He was staring and smiling at what was clearly a long-lost friend, his eyes so full of love and serenity that it was hard for those around him to not be overcome by tears.

Sheila says: "There was no mistake. Someone had come for him at the last to show him the way."

Minutes later the man died, in a state of sublime peace and happiness.

From that day Sheila Mendoza looked upon her dying patients with new eyes and dignity. Like so many others who care for the terminally ill, she had witnessed that precious moment when life slips all ties to a battered, broken body and moves on toward who knows where.

Who was this long-lost family member or friend? Only the dying man will ever know. What is important to recognize is that this reunion somehow prepared him for his death. This vision enabled him to easily pass on to the next stage of existence. It also taught the health-care worker a vital lesson about working with the terminally ill.

The medical community—actually, all of us—can learn many lessons from the dying and DBVs. In the following account, a mother hears from a dying aunt details regarding her deceased daughter's existence in the afterlife. This experience brings this mother a sense of joy and relief. Not only is she reassured that her daughter is well, but the mother quickly recognizes that her dying aunt will also be cared for when she passes.

A few years ago my husband's aunt had a serious stroke and was unconscious in the hospital for a few days. My daughter had died a year or so earlier. I was "speaking" (out loud) to my daughter who had passed and told her it looked like her great aunt would be joining her soon and told her it would be nice if she could visit her. Yes, I'm still a typical mother when it comes to my daughter (even though she is dead).

My mother-in-law and several other family members were at my aunt's side when she suddenly woke up. She wanted to talk about my dead daughter. She said she had seen her. My aunt said that my daughter looked beautiful. She added that she was fine and so very safe. She then said my daughter was with God. The family didn't like hearing this kind of talk and they kept trying to change the subject, but my aunt wanted to continue talking about my daughter. It was strange that she mentioned my daughter, because she had lost other people who were much closer to her. She died two days later. I was glad my mother-in-law shared this with me.

Just one of the innumerable gifts of DBVs is that messages from the dying about other deceased relatives can heal old wounds. Sadly, many of these messages go unheard. Society doesn't yet see these visions as normal. As a result, dying individuals experiencing DBVs are often misdiagnosed, disregarded, ignored, heavily medicated or shut away. Unaware family members often have an extremely difficult time understanding why Dad is talking to Uncle Joe, because Uncle Joe has been dead for twenty years. Many health-care workers dismiss DBVs as hallucinations by telling family members things like,

"Your father is delusional," or "He doesn't know what he is saying."

Hopefully, as time goes on, our culture will gain greater awareness of this phenomena. When such acceptance occurs, more families will greet DBVs as opposed to retreating from them. As was often the case a century ago, visions and otherworldly reunions will once again be viewed as a benefit to all present at the deathbed. For example, the following deathbed reunion was very enlightening for one of America's most famous spiritual leaders.

Evangelist Dr. Billy Graham was with his grandmother the day she died. According to a quote in George Gallup Jr.'s work, *Adventures in Immortality* (1983), Graham's grandmother, who had been very weak, suddenly sat up and announced she was seeing her deceased husband, Ben. Dr. Graham's grandfather fought in the Civil War and had lost a leg and an eye during battle. Just before she died, Graham's grandmother said, "There is Ben, and he has both of his eyes and both of his legs!"

The grandmother left this world with a sense of exaltation at seeing her beloved husband whole and healed. The vision must have also been very comforting to Dr. Graham. Today, Dr. Graham is one of the most revered spiritual leaders in the United States. What impact might this particular DBV have had on Dr. Graham's concept of life after death?

When a dying person has a DBV, surrounding family members are often better able to let go of their loved one. One beautiful DBV account comes from a delightful woman named Gladys. In this touching account, Gladys encourages her beloved husband to leave his ill body. Her husband's DBV made the dying process easier on both of them.

My husband Bryan died of cancer on August 29, 1995. With help from the local hospice, he was allowed to come home two weeks before his death. We had been married for forty-four years and had our share of spats, but never once did either of us feel unloved. I like to call that last two weeks (before he died) our last "honeymoon." We were very open with the fact that he was dying, and we talked at great lengths about heaven and if we would know each other when I got there.

An attendant, Morris, was hired to come in and help me on Mondays from 9 A.M. to 5 P.M. The first thing I asked Morris to do in the mornings was change Bryan's bed. Since Bryan had bone cancer, any movement was painful. During the final hours of his life, I was standing at the foot of the bed while Morris was moving Bryan. As Morris moved him he said, "Bryan, I am trying to be easy with you," to which Bryan responded, "Don't sweat the little things."

Then Bryan looked straight at me and said, "Mama! Mama!" I knew at that time he was not seeing me, but his mother who was waiting for him in heaven. I also knew the moment his body died that an angel had come to take his soul home. He died at 4:15 the next morning. . . . I rubbed his head and told him to please let go and go to God. . . . I had given him the greatest of love by asking God to take his hand and lead him home. . . . (Bryan was) the greatest man that ever lived in my life.

For those preparing to travel to the other side of the veil, recognizing that family members are waiting must be extremely reassuring. Science unfortunately continues to downplay DBVs. In this age of science, popular belief holds that we die alone. My father-in-law was for years a firm believer in the rigid laws of science. When the topic of life after death would come up in conversation, Pop would say, "We become worm food and that is it! Lights out! We just expire! The end!" I bet he was surprised when he ended up in an afterlife world!

Parenting from Beyond

Many of the DBVs I've documented relate to contact with parents and parent figures who have died. The next DBV was taken from *Psychic Research and the Resurrection* by J. H. Hyslop (1908). This absolutely beautiful narrative was given by a Dr. Wilson of New York. Dr. Wilson was at the deathbed of famous American tenor James Moore. The account is well known among DBV researchers.

It was about four o'clock and the dawn for which he had been waiting was creeping in through the shutters, when, as I bent over the bed, I noticed his face was quite calm and his eyes clear. The poor fellow looked up into my face, and taking my hand in both of his, he said, "You've been a good friend to me, Doctor. You've stood by me." Then something which I shall never forget to my dying day happened, something which is utterly indescribable. While he appeared perfectly rational and as sane as any man I have ever seen, the only way that I can express it is that he was transported into another world, and although I cannot satisfactorily explain the matter to myself, I am fully convinced that he entered the Golden City, for he said in a stronger voice than he had used since I attended him, "There is Mother! Why, Mother, have you come to see me? No, no, I'm coming to see you. Just wait Mother, I'm almost over. I can jump it. Wait, Mother." On his face there was a look of inexpressible happiness, and the way in which he said the words impressed me as I have never been before, and I am (as) firmly convinced that he saw and talked with his mother as I am that I am sitting here.

In order to preserve what I believe to be his conversation with his (deceased) mother, and also to have a record of the strangest happening of my life, I immediately wrote down every word he said. . . . His was one of the most beautiful deaths I have ever seen.

Across the unknown, one more mother comes to escort her beloved child to the next world, as if the maternal instinct to protect offspring continues after the physical body has disintegrated. With the passage of time and boundaries of death, motherly love can continue. I recently received the following DBV account of a one-hundred-year-old woman who had a blessed visit from her mother just before she passed.

My mother died in 1976. Her sister-in-law died a few years later, one week prior to her one hundredth birthday. For about a week before her death (she was not ill and was perfectly lucid at all times), she began giving daily announcements to the family about visits with her mother. This, I say, happened every day. She died peacefully at the end of the week.

' A call from Mom from the beyond! Is this only an American phenomena or is it a cross-cultural experience? The next account answers this question. The following DBV comes from Osis and Haraldsson's collection of deathbed visions in *At the Hour of Death*. Here, a young Hindu boy is passing. The nurses and doctors at his deathbed shared this vision with Dr. Osis.

He often talked about (his mother). . . . He mentioned her . . . very affectionately. The day he died he had no fever but he said, "My time has come" to his father. "My mother is calling. She is standing with her arms open." At that moment his state of mind was clear. He was conscious of his surroundings and talked to his father until the last moment. Then, with one hand holding his father's and the other pointed toward where he saw his mother, he said, "Don't you see Mother? See!. . . Then he died, stretching forward to [her] . . . almost falling out of bed. He was so happy to see her!

Most mothers want to be there for their children, as though the desire to "mother" continues in the afterlife. To see what I mean, read the next account.

My sister had cancer and was living out her last days at home. Every time I walked past her room, she seemed to be talking to someone. One day, I was outside her bedroom door and I heard her ask for a glass of water, so I went to get her one. When I took it into her room, she looked at me and said, "Oh, thank you. You didn't have to bring it. I had already asked Mom to bring me a drink."

Our mother had been dead for years, so I asked her who she had been talking with. She said she had been talking to our mother!

What is so interesting about these visions is not only their impact on the dying, but their effect on those who previously would never have even considered such visitations possible. The dying man in the following narrative appears to be totally surprised with the sudden appearance of his mother-in-law.

My mother lived with us throughout our marriage. A few months ago, my husband—who I must say does not believe in any of these kind of experiences—told me that my [deceased] mom was in the house. It would take something very dramatic for my husband to make such a statement.

As the moment of death draws near, nonbelievers are often surprised with a DBV. The man in the previous example never would have expected his mother-in-law to return from the dead. Imagine his astonishment when he realized his mother-in-law was revisiting her old stomping grounds!

When my time to die arrives, I strongly suspect my mother, who died many years ago, will return to my side, and I have often wondered what our reunion will be like. Knowing my mother, if she does visit my deathbed, she will probably tell me how to die! You think I'm joking? Read the following DBV report, in which a dying woman receives specific directions from a deceased mate on what to do at the moment of death.

On February 14 my mother said to the nurse, "Today is Valentine's Day. Too bad my husband can't be with me. Perhaps I will see him today." She later said my dad came to see her and said that she will see a bright light and to turn right and he will be there waiting for her. Then she said that she needed to get ready to die and began to pray and sing.

My belief is that the personality continues after death. If someone is loving in this life, who's to say they won't be loving in the next existence? If a husband had provided support and assistance to his wife while alive, it only makes sense this pattern of behavior would continue after death.

Family Affairs

While visiting with Raymond Moody, the famous NDE researcher, I contacted a number of deceased relatives. I saw them in spirit form and several of them actually touched me. The feeling of love was overwhelming. My communication was both visual and sensory, and it took some time to sort it out. Seeing the spirits of deceased loved ones was a new experience, and I needed a great deal of space to reflect on it. After reviewing my contact with the other side, I quickly understood I was not alone on this earth. In spite of death, my loving, deceased family members continue to reach out to me. Do such family reunions also take place at the moment of death?

In the following DBV account—taken by Barrett (1926) from *Reminiscence* by Alfred Smedley—the author shares with us his wife's departing words. In this particular account, the whole family shows up to escort her to the other side. When I first read this account, I thought, *Gee! I can sure relate!* This DBV truly was a family affair.

A short time before her decease, her eyes being fixed on something that seemed to fill her with pleasant surprise, she exclaimed, "Why! There is sister Charlotte here, and Mother and Father, and brother John and sister Mary! And now they have brought Bessie Heap!! They are all here. Oh! How beautiful! Cannot you see them?" she asked. "No, dear; I very much wish I could," I answered. "Can you not see them?" she again asked in surprise. "Why, they are all here, and they are come to bear me away with them!" Then she added, "Part of our family have crossed the flood, and soon the other part will be gathered home, and then we shall be a family complete in heaven!"

I may explain here that Bessie Heap had been the trusted family nurse, and my wife had always been a favorite with her.

After the above ecstatic experience, my wife lingered for some time. Then fixing her gaze steadily upward again, and lifting up her hands, she joined the convoy of angel friends, who had come to usher her into that brighter spiritual world of which we had learned so little.

Having a number of deceased family members show up during a visitation can be a joy for both the dying and for the surviving family. Talk about a reunion! In the next account, a dying woman has a visitation from not only her living children, but from one son she hasn't seen in many years.

My grandmother had seven children, the second of which was a boy, her first son. This was around 1920. This child died when he was only fourteen months old. My grand-mother grieved over the loss of this child her whole life. In 1965, as she was dying, her six living children were standing around her bed. Looking up at them, she pointed to each one of them and spoke to them. She also pointed out a seventh child and spoke with him. She was speaking to the little boy who had died so many years ago. Obviously, she was the only one who could see him.

For the woman in the above example, her reunion with her oldest son was a joyous occasion. In the next account, the desire to leap across the bridge separating this world from the next was embraced after a family meeting!

Before my grandfather died, he mentioned seeing his mother, my grandmother, my aunt and a couple of cousins. All of these relatives were deceased.

A reunion with numerous deceased relatives appears to have a positive effect on the dying. To see relatives who were once thought to be long gone must be such a delight. In the next recent day account, a deceased sister makes an unusual visit.

My mother-in-law saw her sister a few days before she passed on. Her sister had passed on years before. She told me her sister had come for coffee!

In interviewing those who have watched a loved one have a DBV, I have found that these family reunions tend to dramatically lessen the fear of death for the survivors. After such an event, surviving family members sense that just across some invisible threshold can be found a safe Shangri-la to which their loved one will travel. With such knowledge comes the recognition that when their time comes, they too will eventually travel to this tended place.

On some occasions, I have found that those at the deathbed are often very interested in the visions their loved ones are having. In such situations, the experience isn't seen as something to fear, but an opportunity to communicate with long-lost relatives. Questions are asked about others who have passed on. Sometimes an answer is received. In the following account, one woman was so interested in her mother's DBV that she asked for more information.

> *My mother died in September 1998. Shortly before she passed, she said to me, "I was just talking to our Anna." Anna was my aunt who had died a year before. I became so interested in her visitation that I asked, "Did you see my brother?" He had recently died and I thought if she had seen Anna, maybe she had seen my brother. Sadly, she replied, "No, I didn't see him." After this she went to sleep and shortly after that my mother passed. My one big regret is that I didn't ask my mother what my aunt had said.*

In the above case, this adult child was drawn into what her mother was seeing during a DBV experience. Though she didn't receive the answer she was searching for, she did take from the experience many lessons that would stay with her for the rest of her life.

Unfortunately, some family members are so fearful of death that they won't explore a loved one's DBVs. What's more, they tend to frantically work at keeping the dying from leaving their physical bodies, even if the final days on earth are racked with illness and pain.

Raymond Moody's groundbreaking book *Life After Life* relates an interesting and amusing DBV case. In this particular situation, a niece's prayers for her elderly aunt become a big problem! The aunt is ready to die, but she feels the family prayers are keeping her bound to her body and she is not happy about this. Here is what the niece reported to Moody:

> *She looked at me and said, "Joan, I have been over there, over to the beyond and it is beautiful over there. I want to stay, but I can't as long as you keep praying for me to stay with you. Your prayers are holding me over here. Please don't pray anymore." We did all stop and shortly after that she died.*

The power of prayer! Yes, the prayers of family and friends can have a great deal of impact on the dying process of a dear one. Praying for family members to not die when they need to go does not serve the departing loved one. Relatives who are fearful of death often cause the dying to feel guilty about wanting to move on and cause them also to hang on in misery. If our loved ones are ready to go, we need to release them. Giving them permission to die eases the death experience for them.

When with an ill person, my prayer is "God's will be done." I keep it that simple. If a friend or loved one appears to be in pain and seriously ill, my prayer is, "Please support this person in a way that will benefit them physically, emotionally and spiritually." While sitting at a deathbed, my silent prayer goes something like this, "May the veil between this world and the next be slightly parted so that [the dying person] can receive visitors from the other side. May these loved ones help to make the transition easier." After praying such a prayer, I have often sensed the presence of a deceased relative.

In my research, I have discovered that while a dying one is having a DBV, family members often have the impression that deceased relatives are near. Look at the following account of how a dying woman's DBV affects her niece.

My great-aunt was nearing the end. . . . I had been with her for days, trying to make her as comfortable as possible. . . . She had not had the energy to speak for over a week. One morning, she started weakly calling out for Ted, her brother, who was my grandfather. Ted had died when my mother was very little, so my contact with him had only been through pictures. My great-aunt called his name softly over and over again

*for about an hour. She was not restless or agitated. She just
kept calling for him.*

*Suddenly, I could sense a presence in the room, over by
her dresser. It wasn't frightening or silly as you would
expect a ghost to be. I instinctively knew it was my grandfather. Within minutes, my great-aunt was gone! It was just
as if he had come to get her and take her home. It was the
most incredible thing I have ever been through!*

Sensing the presence of departed loved ones has been
documented time and time again by ADC researchers.
When my grandmother died, for weeks afterwards I would
regularly feel her presence while in my kitchen cooking! I
just knew she was there. The sensation was incredibly
strong. She was an excellent cook and had taught me how
to prepare many of the ethnic Russian-German dishes I
had grown up eating. After overcoming the surprise of her
initial social call, I found my grandmother's periodic visits
quite comforting.

The Stare

Since I started collecting accounts of DBVs, family members have often asked me about another deathbed phenomena
known as the "Stare." Because we are talking about family
matters, I feel I should briefly discuss the transfixed gaze
the dying often have as death approaches. This experience is

terribly misunderstood and, if not properly addressed, can leave surviving family members frightened.

As my mother's mother was dying, she was obviously having a hard time. Because I was very young and unaware, I found her last few hours extremely frightening. In my family, nobody talked to me about my grand-mother's death, and because of this, her dying process just seemed awful.

Through the fear and tears, I did note something inter-esting about her passing. As my grandmother left her frail body, her eyes were fixated on the ceiling. No matter what was happening around her (doctors, nurses, IVs, crying relatives) her gaze appeared to be following something on the ceiling of her hospital room. When I asked the medical help and other adults around me, "What is she looking at?" I was told, "Your grandmother is not looking at anything. She's dying. That's why she looks that way!" After hearing the adult take on all of this, I remember thinking, "Okay, so this is just the way death is." It would be many years before I would give my grandmother's fixed stare another thought.

In studying DBVs, I discovered other individuals who had also witnessed this intense gaze. While listening to many people share about this, I thought, *I bet my grandmother was seeing something! She just wasn't able to verbalize it! Both her children had passed on. I wonder if they came to get her?* After pondering various accounts of this nature, I am convinced that many of these dying individuals are seeing deceased loved ones, but for one reason or another, the dying are unable to share the visions. The following account is a great example of the fixated DBV stare.

> *Death is nothing to be feared. . . . Mom was in intensive care a week before she died. . . . She was staring, her eyes transfixed on the ceiling. I have no idea of what she saw, but the look on her face told me it was beautiful. I spoke to her and she looked in my direction once, only to turn and stare back at the ceiling with a smile on her face.*

Why did this woman respond to her daughter with only a brief look and then turn to stare at the ceiling? What was she seeing? It is obvious that this vision gave the mother great joy because she was smiling. Another similar account displays this particular phenomena.

> *My father was so afraid of dying. He was really fighting it. My father slipped into a coma and we waited for him to pass. Shortly before he died, he calmed down. He looked straight past me and smiled at whatever (or whoever) he saw. Then he peacefully let his spirit go.*

Here we have a man who is fighting death. He is terrified! Suddenly he has a vision of something that no one else in the room can see. With this, he is comforted and he gently passes. What relieved his fear of death? What did he see? Who gently reassured him he would be all right? In the next account, we are told a young boy is dying. As he makes his way to the other side, he too sees something that is not visible to others in the room.

After four hours of our son just laying there as if sleeping, he suddenly opened his eyes and sat straight up. The room he was in was very small. We were the only ones in this room with our son and we were sitting right next to his bed. When he sat up, he looked directly at the foot of his bed. Then he looked to each side of his bed with a look of question. After this, he gently laid back down. . . . Then his breath started to go. . . .

After reading this account, one wonders just how many visitors this young man had during this vision. Not only did he look intently at the foot of his bed, but then looked to each side of the bed. I wonder what he was questioning?

Deathbed visitors come in both sexes and all ages. In researching DBVs, I am often asked why one particular image doesn't visit everyone. I believe the dying receive visitations from those special friends who are best qualified to assist them to the other side.

In the next account we have a vision seen by a fourteen-year-old boy dying of consumption. For this

youngster, an elderly visitor brings comfort. This account
is taken from Barrett's collection of DBVs (1926).

> *On the morning of the day he died, his mother—having*
> *left the room to fetch him something—heard him call and*
> *hastened back, found him sitting up in bed, looking towards*
> *the corner of the room, and he said to her, "There is a nice*
> *old man come for me; he is holding out his arms for me. I*
> *must go. Don't fret, Mother," and he fell back gently on his*
> *pillow and was gone, without any struggle for breath, and*
> *with a smile of joy on his face which remained.*

Next is the account of a mother who was admitted to the
hospital for what initially was thought to be only an infec-
tion. Within a few days of her admission, her illness turns
out to be a more serious condition. Her daughter had been
on vacation, but the mother waited for her to return before
she passed.

> *Everything was fine all week long. We spoke to her (while*
> *vacationing) every day. . . . She was doing great, up reading,*
> *walking and everything. After we spoke to her Thursday*
> *morning, that night she started to decline and began to get*
> *that "deathbed stare," that wide-eyed, strange look, kind of*
> *like in amazement. By the time I saw her, I could tell she*
> *was slowly slipping away. I spent all day Sunday with her.*
> *She just kept staring at the same spot in the room, at the*
> *ceiling—as if she was looking at someone or something.*
> *Her lips would move but no words were coming out of*

her mouth. She kept saying "Denise." We had no clue as to who Denise was. None of her nurses were named Denise and we are still researching this. Along with this, she kept wanting to get out of bed and would say, "I have to go!" It was as if she had to go somewhere. When we asked where she had to go, she would mumble, "You just don't understand."

This happened a few times. Each time it did, we laid her back down and she would then again stare at the same spot up by the ceiling. This went on all day. Before we left that day, my sister, me, my brother and my dad had to tell her it was okay to die. The next day, a Monday, we arrived at twelve. At 1:22 she simply winced, and then whispered what appeared to be the words, "Love ya." Then her breathing just simply stopped. All the pain was over. She was finally at peace.

It was so peaceful to watch her pass. It felt like a weight had been lifted. I am so happy she waited for us to get back from vacation. It's like she knew we were on our way home and that it was okay to start to go. Funny how things happen, huh? I am not afraid to die now!

Once again we have a woman who is seeing "something" but in this case, she is concerned that her family will not understand. I have often wondered if more DBVs occur than are reported. Do many of those who are passing have visions but choose to not share them? Are they afraid we will not understand? Here is one final account of the stare. Compare it with those previously presented.

> *I am sure my mom was having visions of someone, something or maybe more than one. She would fix her eyes on one particular corner of the room and be so totally into whatever it was she was watching. She would turn her head as if following an object.*
>
> *My mom stayed very calm during these periods, which would last for about five to ten minutes. Then we could see her lay back and relax. She was living with us before she died, and I saw her do this at least four times.*
>
> *I am convinced it was something very spiritual, and I am so happy she experienced it and that we (my husband, son and I) experienced it with her.*

In all of these cases, it appears as though the person who is making the transition from this life to the afterlife sees a vision that nobody else in the room can comprehend. The stare is fixated on something or someone, and the gaze appears to follow. These visions provide the dying with a sense of calm, peace and reassurance. Before my grandmother passed, she was unable to speak. If she had been able to talk, I wonder what she would have said. Did my mother, uncle and great-grandparents come for her? Was that who she was looking at? Did she have a family reunion? I sure hope so.

DBVs bring a great deal of psychological and spiritual

peace to both the dying and their family members. Deceased relatives returning to escort the dying to the other side provide a sense of continuity. Life goes on here and there; the housing situation is just a little different. These family reunions are a true blessing.

Chapter 5

Visitations from Special Friends

"Does nobody understand me?"

Parting words of James Joyce

Visitations from deceased friends and loved ones come in all forms. As we have seen, they can appear visually to the dying and their family. In other instances, they will show up in dreams. Some visitations present themselves as strong psychic images.

Several years ago, a number of friends of mine all died within a relatively short period of time. One of these individuals, who I will refer to as Rose, had been ill for some time. She was a great gal and I always enjoyed her company. Long on opinions, Rose always had a comment about everything. When she finally passed, something very unusual began to happen. I started to psychically hear her laughing. Time and time again, my thoughts would be interrupted by Rose's laughter. It didn't matter if I was watching television, in the shower or sitting with my boys. Here would come this loud, raucous laugh.

While she was alive, I had never heard her laugh in this boisterous manner. Because of this, I started to wonder just where these impressions were coming from. Finally, after three days of these outbursts, I decided to visualize her and ask, "What is so damn funny?" Immediately, the message I received was, "What a joke! We don't die! I'm still here!" This was followed by a huge belly laugh. Rose appeared to be totally surprised to see life continued, and for some reason she thought this was just hysterical. After several more days of this pervasive laughter, suddenly there was silence. Once Rose's laughter ceased, it never returned.

For several months, I reflected on this experience. It wasn't at all frightening, but initially the laughter had been most confusing. As time went by, I began to feel immense gratitude for the experience. Before moving on to the afterlife, my special friend Rose had chosen to visit me. She and I had shared one last, intimate moment together.

For years I didn't openly discuss this encounter with anyone. As a matter of fact, I would often tell Michael, "If I shared this with people 'out there,' they will say I'm nuts, psychotic, hallucinating or just plain crazy. And forget my buddies in the health-care professions. All they would say is 'hush,' or 'keep quiet about such things.' Nobody would ever understand this!"

MEDICAL COMMUNITY PERSPECTIVES

Visitations from special, otherworldly friends are often kept private. Most doctors, nurses, psychiatrists, psychologists and other health-care practitioners have great difficulty hearing about such matters. Instead of using such visions to spiritually and emotionally soothe grieving family members or dying clients, these experiences are quickly dismissed. Health-care professionals tend to hastily disregard the healing balm DBVs or other paranormal experiences can provide.

An encounter with deceased relatives, light beings or angels appears to bring a dying person a great sense of relief and peace. In many cases, the individual who is passing is the only one who sees these visitors. Because of this, family, friends and caregivers often ignore these experiences, seeing them as mere hallucinations. Even when the person receiving such a vision is lucid and aware of physical surroundings, medical personnel commonly write up a prescription for anxiety or even psychosis. As James Joyce said before passing, "Does nobody understand me?"

In many hospital settings, the dying are often discouraged

from talking about their visions. Most job descriptions for medical health-care workers call for prolonging life, not ending it. Assisting patients toward a peaceful death runs counter to this presumption. Also, many doctors and nurses often feel uncomfortable with the dying process. Several doctors have actually told me when their patients die, they feel like "failures."

When my father-in-law was in the hospital, his physician was very young and seemed to have a phobia about death. In spite of the fact that Pop had suffered a major stroke and was obviously making the death transition, at night the medical staff continued to give him blood infusions. Family members were furious. After that point, my husband, sister, mother-in-law and kids decided to plant ourselves at his bedside, twenty-four hours a day. We wanted Pop to be able to make his big exit with a sense of honor.

Sadly, many people in society are forced to die without dignity, alone in sterile hospital rooms. Strict visitation hours keep family away, and the constant pursuit of "life" by the medical staff can make dying a miserable experience. Every once in a while, a family confronting death is blessed with the wisdom and compassion of a doctor or nurse who truly is aware of the spiritual nature of dying. When this happens, DBVs can be accepted and used for the good of all involved. The following account provides us with a beautiful example of how medical personnel can use these visions to positively assist in the dying process.

Our son passed over on August 4, 1997. I believe he did have deathbed visions. The first one happened after he had a seizure. His heart stopped, and after he came back to life, he seemed all right. But then he looked at me and said, "Mom, what happened to me?" I didn't want to scare him, so I told him he had fainted. He replied, "Whatever happened to me was wonderful! It felt so good! I liked that!"

When my husband visited with the doctor he told him what our son had said. The doctor said to him, "You do know that what your son experienced was a near-death experience."

When the second vision took place, my son had been unconscious for over an hour. Suddenly, he sat up in an upright position! This happened very quickly. We were so shocked, we didn't say a word to him. We thought, "My God, he came out of it!" so we just sat and stared.

He looked toward the foot of his bed and then up. He was looking as though he were seeing more than one person. He turned his head slightly from side to side. The look on his face was like he was confused with what he was staring at. Then, after a few minutes, he laid back down and looked very peaceful. He returned to his unconscious state and at this point all we could do was hold him. Not long after that, our son went into cardiac arrest and passed on.

When this boy's heart stopped, he was at a point of death. Though death was near, he was not ready to leave his physical body for good. During this interval, he had a vision. A friend of mine also had such an experience during surgery. Many people have reported visions—near-death experiences or NDEs—when their hearts were not beating and for all clinical purposes they were dead.

In the previous account, the boy was able to catch a glimpse of another world during an NDE. When he came out of his unconscious state, he had a DBV. These two occurrences assured this boy's parents that he would be happy and safe on the other side. The doctor's acknowledgment of the NDE clarified and validated the experience for the grieving parents. Such clarification must have eased the parents' pain. The doctor provided the surviving family with a true gift.

Claudio and Nicola

A good friend of mine employed in the medical profession shows incredible tenderness toward those who are passing. When a dying patient or family member presents him with a DBV, he is quick to validate their experience. Where did he learn to have such compassion and understanding? Several years ago, a personal loss taught Claudio about the importance of DBVs. During this time he was introduced to visitors from the other side. The lesson began when his beloved son Nicola was diagnosed with a rare form of childhood cancer.

* * *

Claudio Pisani is a forty-seven-year-old medical doctor living in Laria, Italy. He is a gregarious fellow, full of life and laughs. Claudio and his family are Catholic and appear devoted to their religion. When I am really down in the dumps, Claudio will send me an e-mail that just sends me screaming with hysterical laughter.

Not very long ago, Claudio and his lovely wife of twenty-two years had a hard time laughing. At that time life rotated around the illness of their six-year-old son. At the time of his initial cancer diagnosis in 1991, Nicola was only three years old. This young boy bravely endured numerous chemotherapies and cancer treatments. One month before his passing he also withstood a grueling month of radiation therapy.

During a second surgery, Nicola suffered heart failure. Once revived, he told his parents that he had seen Jesus walking "over the floor" and that he had spoken with his guardian angel.

Initially, Claudio and his wife thought Nicola was imagining things. At that time, the vision was not discussed in depth. Two weeks later, Nicola's visions of the guardian angel began to increase and the boy was praying to this angel daily. Early one morning, on an Easter Sunday, Nicola's parents found him staring out a window. Not only was he intently looking at something, but he was having a conversation. Here is what Claudio had to say about that morning.

> *My Nicola was looking out a window near his bed and he suddenly said, "No!... please ... wait ... go away ... no, go away, no more ... another little bit of time." He was talking to someone, but I wasn't able to see who. Nicola was awake and he wasn't in a coma. My son wasn't delirious or on any strong medications like morphine or other related drugs.*
>
> *Previous to this conversation, he had not been eating and his temperature was very low. Once his conversation with this vision ended, he asked for a cup of milk! After that he told us he was talking to his guardian angel regularly and used glowing terms to describe him. Two weeks after this, he died.*

For some reason, little Nicola needed a bit more time before he passed. What is so interesting about this particular DBV is that before his conversation with the guardian angel, the six-year-old boy did not want to eat. Once the dialogue ended, he requested a glass of milk. Claudio truly believes his son wanted to spend several more days with him and his wife and that this was what he was requesting from the angel in his vision.

The Blessing of Hospice

In recent years, hospices—organizations consisting of medical personnel and volunteer staff trained to assist not only the dying, but family members—have become increasingly popular in the United States. Educated to understand the deathbed vision phenomena, these health-care givers can assure the dying and family members that this experience is normal. As opposed to being seen as a curse in need of medication, the DBV can be embraced as a blessing. Several years ago, two hospice nurses, Maggie Callanan and Patricia Kelley, put out their own form of the *Book of the Dead* entitled *Final Gifts* (1997). The manual assists health-care workers in understanding the many different facets of dying.

During the last few days of Pop's life, my family and I turned to hospice. Being surrounded by medical staff who understood the dying process was a godsend. Each of the hospice workers assigned to Pop's case had been trained in the physical and emotional aspects of dying. Unlike traditional doctors and nurses, who delay death for as long as possible, hospice medical teams view death as a normal process. They believe the dying should be allowed to leave this world with dignity, love and support.

The difference between hospice health-care providers and many of the death-phobic doctors at hospitals can be radical. For hospice personnel, DBVs and NDEs are seen as a bridge to the afterlife. Instead of dismissing such experiences, hospice workers use them to make the transition of dying a more positive experience for everyone involved.

With hospice and books like *Final Gifts,* in the future more and more medical personnel should be better prepared to offer compassion and assistance to the dying and their families.

Religious Visitations

My research often uncovers reports of visions of angels, God or other religious figures. These familiar sights appear to make the dying process less frightening. Nicola saw Jesus walking across the floor and then had visions of a guardian angel, which reassured both of his parents.

The following DBV account comes from my research.

I remember as a very small girl being in the room with my mom and aunt as my uncle was dying. He was a gruff sort of person, but as my aunt was tending the fire in the fireplace, he said, "Who is that beautiful lady beside you?"

She said, "There's no one here."

He said, "Yes, there is. She's on your right (and he pointed). She's all in white and she is very beautiful."

He died shortly thereafter.

Who was this beautiful lady dressed in all white? Was she an angel? What a lovely vision this woman in white must have been. This gentle DBV could erase any fear of death and would make passing a peaceful blessing.

Here is another DBV with not only a comforting religious figure, but a second unknown visitor.

> *My father had deathbed visions. He talked of a man who was in the room. My father said that he had conversations with this man about how he was feeling. He also told us he was talking with God. The night he did make his transition, my mother and my husband had been up to see him. My mother told him they would be back the next day to visit. My father told her there wasn't enough time. At first she didn't know what he meant, but later she did, because he had died that night.*

None of the family knew the "man" with whom their ailing father was communicating. Regardless, the family realized that these conversations brought their father great peace. At one point, the father states that he has also been talking with "God." Calmed by these visions, he is able to tell his family he is powerless to wait for their visit the following day. He says he cannot wait because there isn't "enough time." Sadly, the family doesn't understand the comment until after the father's passing. Thankfully, not all is lost. Recognizing he understood death was near, and that he felt he had loving escorts to assist him to the other side, eventually brought his family a great sense of peace. When fear of death is removed, the dying are free to let go.

Let's look at another DBV involving a visit from God.

My husband was in the hospital following surgery. He was in cardiac intensive care. On Friday morning, he wrote me a note and said that "God came into my life last night." He died on Saturday.

Osis and Haraldsson also reported religious figures seen during a DBV. The religious figures who were seen usually related to the dying person's religion. At first glance, such visions may be confusing, not only to survivors, but to researchers. A question that is often asked is, why do specific religious figures appear to certain dying people? At the moment of death, why don't the same religious figures appear to everyone across the board? In the next account, the woman relating the vision provides us with an excellent explanation. Note that the dying boy is close to the narrator's parents; he calls her mother Mom.

Sadly, this young boy was very ill and died of leukemia at the age of eleven. Before he died he told my mother, "I saw Peter."

My mother said, "Peter who?"

With a smirk on his face, he said, "You know what Peter." It was then that the nurse told my mother he meant St. Peter.

A few days later the boy awoke crying from a dream. "St. Peter threw away the key! He threw away the key!" In his dream, he saw St. Peter throw away the keys to heaven, and he (the boy) was inside.

He had one wish, to be home for Christmas. Well, that young boy lived till Christmas Eve. That night, my mother had a dream that the boy came to say "Good-bye, Mom" and then turned and walked away, hand in hand with his father. My mother yelled to him, "Come back!" Then she was awakened by the ringing of the telephone, to inform her that the young boy had died.

It doesn't matter what religion you are. I believe the higher powers let us see what we can understand, and in this case, for this little boy, it was St. Peter.

I agree that when the dying are passing, they are visited by those who will comfort them during their travel to the other side. For a dying Christian, that might mean Jesus; a Buddhist may see Buddha. For others, an angel, a beautiful woman or Druid priest would bring more comfort. If I'm following a particular philosophy of religion, wouldn't it make sense for me to be visited at the moment of my death by an otherworldly escort who is familiar with my belief system? The following story comes from a woman who had a son in the same hospital as the aforementioned eleven-year-old boy. Once again we have another encounter with a religious figure.

My mother told me she had met a woman in the hospital. The woman told my mother that her son, who was then three years old, had come to her with a compelling tale. Her son said, "Mommy, he said he was taking me on a vacation." The son then pointed upwards towards the wall. There hung a crucifix of Jesus Christ.

Recently, my aunt Lena June gave me the following DBV account. Her mother had been very ill for many years. Before she crossed over, she too was visited by Jesus. As her death neared, this is what happened.

My mother was so ill. Bless her heart, it was difficult to watch. One day my sister was sitting with her. She was resting comfortably when suddenly she started speaking out loud in German. Though she was originally from Germany, she didn't often speak in her mother tongue. Anyway, after talking in German for a while, she turned to my sister and said, "Don't worry about me. Everything is going to be just fine! I just had a talk with Jesus and there is nothing to worry about. Everything will be all right!" After this, she spoke in German for a bit longer. A short time later she lapsed into a coma and then passed on fifteen days later.

Lena June's dying mother tried to reassure her daughter that she would be "all right." Her DBV had given her peace, and she wanted to pass this on to Lena June. My aunt said that her mother's vision brought her great comfort and eased the loss of the passing. In the following DBV account, though, the man receiving the vision isn't completely comfortable with his visitors. As he becomes more familiar with them, his attitude slowly changes.

The last week of my brother's life, I was visiting him. As I walked into his bedroom, he said, "I wish those people would go away. They are scaring me!"

I then asked, "Where are these people?"

My brother pointed to the corner of the room and said, "They are standing right there."

I asked him, "If they are scaring you, why don't you just ask them to leave?"

My brother replied, "I don't want to ask them to leave because I think they are angels. I don't think they are supposed to leave."

Though the aforementioned visit was initially frightening, he knew that the "angels" were supposed to be there. What is also interesting is that intuitively he appears to have even known who they were. I suspect this person might have been a bit fearful of the visitation because he knew this meant his moment of departure was near. Hopefully as time went on, the visiting angels lessened his fear. As is often the case, the dying man did not describe for his surviving family just what these angels looked like. When such details are left out of an account, surviving family members can feel confused or unsure of the vision.

Unlike this gentleman, a very dear friend of mine was not afraid of death at all. For years, we lived next door to an elderly Southern gentleman. Every time I baked cookies or cakes for my family, I always took a portion over to my neighbor. He absolutely loved sweets, especially warm, just-out-of-the-oven chocolate chip cookies! He lived a very long life. As a matter of fact, when he turned one hundred years old, he made it a point of putting on a suit and hat and then walked around the block! He just had to prove he could still do it!

When he hit 105 years of age, he was very ready to pass. One morning he woke up and said, "Why won't Jesus come take me away? I sure do wish Jesus would come and get me!" By noon that day, our delightful neighbor had passed. Obviously someone, somewhere had heard his plea!

In the following DBV account, a guardian angel visits the dying.

Right before my Dad passed away, he started seeing a man that only he could see. My Dad called him "John." He would ask my mom if she could see him, and of course she couldn't. John was with my dad every day for the week before he died. He would say that John was with him from the time he woke up until he went to sleep that night. I think that John was my dad's guardian angel and that he was there to help my dad over to the other side.

EXPERIENCES THAT STARTLE

Most DBVs bring comfort to the dying, but some visions can actually startle unsuspecting family members. The presence of visiting deceased relatives and special friends often creates a great deal of confusion for these unaware surviving loved ones. Because people at the bedside may not see what the dying are seeing, they can find themselves in trouble! Here is another vision taken from Barrett (1926). Notice how upset the dying woman is with her sister for not seeing what she sees.

> *Some years ago, I went to see a cousin of mine in Acton who was very ill, and I was told by her sister that on the previous evening, as she sat down on a chair by the bedside, the invalid exclaimed, "Oh, don't, J——! Oh, you have sent mother away, she was sitting there!" and she continued to seem much distressed. My aunt had died some years previously. The dying girl told me about this herself when we were alone.*

In this particular deathbed vision, we have a dying girl who becomes very concerned when her cousin chooses to sit on a chair apparently already occupied by her deceased mother. Read the next DBV story and note the similarities. Then ask yourself, "Are we, the living, lacking in protocol when it comes to dealing with visitors from the other side?"

> *My father, who died in August with terminal brain cancer, began seeing a "little boy" days before he passed. Many times he would say, "Who's that?" or "Don't sit there! You will sit on the little boy!" We decided this was his angel, preparing him for his journey into the hereafter. The DBV*

brought us much joy and peace. He was always delighted to see the little boy. Our hospice agency told us it was common for the terminally ill to see these "angels" before death. He also made a few statements like, "I need to get packed for my trip!" and what a trip he took, to ultimate paradise. What a comfort!

Like the mother in the DBV from Barrett's book, in the last vision, the visiting "little boy" is very real to the dying man, so real that he wants to protect him and make sure no one "sits" on him! This family was blessed to have hospice assistance. Without their guidance and confirmation of this vision, a traditional medical staff might have attributed this man's conversations with the little boy to the brain tumor.

In the following DBV, a visitor is not so easily accepted. As a matter of fact, the dying man questions the visitor's manners! The following account involves an afterlife summons from a very lovely woman.

I was at the nursing home visiting my stepfather. I knew he was going to pass sometime in the future, but didn't think it would happen right away. My stepfather kept referring to the smiling lady who was sitting on the empty bed in the room. Of course, I couldn't see her. He then wondered out loud why this woman was being so rude. My stepfather thought she should leave the room while he and I had our conversation. He found this most confusing. Then he told me, "She always seems so happy." He said this several times to me. I was concerned about this vision he was having and asked the medical staff about it. They assured me that he was stable for the time being. After that, I decided to go and drove home. As I opened the front door to my house, the phone was ringing. My stepfather had died during my short drive to my residence. I used to be very skeptical of such things, but now I know there is more to life than we know.

Multiple Visitors

As we've seen thus far, deathbed visitations manifest themselves in a great variety of ways. Sometimes more than one visitor appears to the dying. Let's look at some examples of DBVs where there are multiple simultaneous visitors. In the first example, a dying man is greeted by several guests.

My husband passed away with kidney cancer fifteen months ago. The cancer had spread to his lungs, brain and bones, leaving him paralyzed for the last several weeks of his life. We kept him at home with the help of hospice until the last few days of his life. During this time, he was usually alert and aware. Two days before he left the house for the hospital, my husband said he saw "people" standing in one corner of the room, up toward the ceiling. Though I could not see them, when he mentioned "those people over there"

we would talk about where they were or who they might be.
He said these people were just standing there, overhead, and
he added that they seemed friendly.

My husband was very aware of them, but he didn't seem
frightened in any way. Also, he didn't find it unusual for
them to be there. I got the distinct feeling that he thought
this was normal, and I think he thought I could see them
too. My husband was someone who questioned everything
(to the point of driving you crazy!) and yet he never tried to
rationalize what he saw. Because of this, I truly believe he
was very clear in what he saw and felt no discomfort in hav-
ing these new "friends."

When the time comes to make the death transition,
some of us appear to need a little more help than others.
My explanation for this phenomenon is built on common
sense. All of us have different needs, especially when we are
getting ready to die. What comforts you might scare me to
death!

At the hour of death, the man in the following example
appears to need more than just one friend. At first his
family thought his visions were the result of his
Alzheimer's disease, but as time went on they changed
their minds.

My in-laws moved in with us when my father-in-law's
Alzheimer's disease became difficult for my mother-in-law
to deal with alone. After he was with us for a while, he was

also diagnosed with lung cancer and was suffering from a heart condition. Before his sickness, he was a most loving and caring person. It was so hurtful to see him this way. One evening, he was very restless and my mother-in-law had been up with him all night.

The next morning, I told her to go and get some sleep. I assured her that I would sit with him while she rested. He was sleeping in his hospital bed as I sat down next to him. As I sat there reading a book, he suddenly sat up and appeared to be looking off into the distance. Then he pointed his finger and said, "There is so and so" (names of people I didn't know) and then he laid back down and went to sleep again. After this, I wondered, is this a symptom of his Alzheimer's or is he going to pass soon? *Somehow I just knew, in the very near future, he would be at peace. He died that evening.*

When this man sat up and started naming off names, was his disease talking or was it something else? Isn't it interesting that none of those he named were known to his daughter-in-law? Was he seeing long-deceased friends who had come to escort him to the other side?

The following DBV brought a sense of serenity to a dying man. Once again, the dying man is not visited by one, but several special visitors.

My father recently died. He had been ill for some time. The radiation therapy he had endured for bladder cancer eventually destroyed his colon and kidneys. He died of renal failure. Three weeks before he passed, he started talking to someone, but we never saw who it was. This would happen when he was napping in the afternoon. During his naps, Mother and I would see him talking away to someone. He would laugh and point his finger, just as if he were having a conversation with someone in the room. One day he even slapped his leg and gave a very hearty laugh.

On another occasion, Mother was sitting next to him while he was asleep and in conversation with someone again. He suddenly woke up and said, "Honey, I'm not afraid to die." This just came out of the clear blue sky! In the weeks that followed, he said this same thing to my mother several times. Toward the end of his life we had to put him back in the hospital. During this time, the nurses would say to me, "He has visitors again." Then they would laugh and add, "They only seem to come when he is asleep."

One evening, I was at his bedside as he was sleeping. I put my hand on his shoulder and he woke up. He looked up at me and said, "Sweetie, we will all be together again, I promise. I love you." Then he turned his head and went back to sleep. Two days later he died. My father was not on any heavy medication because he was not in pain.

This particular DBV provided comfort and reassurance that a dying man and his loved ones would be together someday. The DBV took place while he was sleeping, and many might think he was dreaming. In the next chapter, we will see that DBVs during the dream state are common. For some individuals, the dream realm provides a brief glimpse of what to expect after death. For now, the important point to remember is that several unknown visitors brought this dying man a sense of contentment and joy during his final hours.

* * *

We have seen how special visitors can bring a sense of calm to the deathbed. Instead of fearing death, people blessed with DBVs are able to gracefully leave life behind. Those deceased loved ones, angels or religious figures who are coming to this world—to help pack us up when it is time to move on—are performing what Jews call a "mitzvah." A mitzvah is considered the highest of all good deeds.

I would like to end this chapter with a very special deathbed visitation. The following DBV packs a powerful punch and gives any family confronted with death something to really think about.

Was Walt Whitman Visiting?

Horace Traubel (1858–1919) was a celebrated American poet who wrote in the style of Walt Whitman. The following DBV was originally taken from the journal of *The American Society for Psychical Research* (1921). In this DBV, Traubel is visited by a number of interesting callers.

On the night of September 3rd Horace was very low. I [Mrs. Flora Macdonald Denison] stayed for a few hours with him. Once his eyes rolled; I thought he was dying, but he just wanted me to turn to him. As I did so, he listened and seemed to hear something. Then he said, "I hear Walt's voice, he is talking to me." I said, "What does he say?" He said, "Walt says, 'Come on, come on.'" After a time he said, "Flora, I see them all about me, Bob and Bucke and Walt and the rest."

Colonel Cosgrave had been with Horace in the afternoon and had seen Walt on the opposite side of the bed, and felt his presence. Then Walt passed through the bed and touched the Colonel's hand, which was in his pocket. The contact was like an electric shock. Horace was also aware of Walt's visible presence and said so.

Did the celebrated poet, Walt Whitman, make a deathbed visit to the poet Hourace Traubel to offer him a hand across the boundary of life and death?

Chapter 6

To Dream and to Share

"Now I want to go home."

Dreamworld DBVs

For centuries, dreams have been referred to as a doorway into another world—a psychic, ethereal world where the rules for existence run counter to our everyday way of thinking. Dreams provide a wealth of creative ideas for artists and writers. The concept for *Dr. Jekyll and Mr. Hyde* had its origins in a dream Robert Louis Stevenson had one night. Dream material provided Salvador Dali with an enormous amount of inspiration. William Blake found that dreams stimulated much of his poetic thought. A number of my own book titles have come from dreams.

Most dreams are related to current events. When we have a great deal of anxiety about our children, love life or work, or are just experiencing a bit of everyday stress, we play this out in our dreams. Our dreams enable us to discharge our anxieties, fears and stress. Sometimes our dreams offer us solutions to problems we may be experiencing. Years ago, I was suffering from horrible stomach pains. They lasted for weeks, and I couldn't understand what was causing them. Nothing I did would relieve the pain. One night, I had a peculiar dream. I dreamt that my abdomen was full of "wormlike" creatures. Was this just a ghastly nightmare or an answer to a prayer? Upon awakening, I intuitively knew I had picked up a parasite. *This,* I thought, *is the cause of my stomach pain!* A visit to my doctor validated my self-diagnosis.

Dreams can also give us information about past unresolved issues, such as traumas from emotional, physical or sexual abuse. Such repressed experiences often appear in symbolic form in our dreams.

In ancient times, dreams were thought to be more spiritual in nature. Every dream was viewed as a message, prophecy or warning from the gods. Written interpretation of dreams, found on papyrus in Egypt, dates back to 2000 B.C. Dreams were used to sort out religious, cultural and political issues. Interestingly, most if not all ancient civilizations saw dreams as a way for the spirits of the deceased to speak to the living. Spirit visitations during dream time were viewed as a blessing. Dreams of this nature were highly valued and taken seriously.

Unlike the generations before us, modern Western civilization still has a difficult time grasping the meaning of unusual dreams that occur close to death. When such dreams are reported today, most psychologists and researchers try to interpret these nighttime visions as symbolic of present problems. Many professionals have a difficult time believing that dreams about loved ones who are dying or already crossed over are anything more than a by-product of grief. In some cases these professionals may be right. But for a select category of dreams—those having DBV or even after-death communication (ADC) characteristics—I personally feel such caregivers are dead wrong. Let's take a look at what such a dream might look like.

My paternal grandmother's death brought me much distress. After my own mother passed, she essentially raised me, and the two of us were very close. When my grandmother died, I was very grateful she was no longer suffering, but I still missed her terribly. One night, before I went to sleep, I asked her to come visit me in a dream. Once asleep, I did dream of her. As usual, she was elegantly dressed. (My grandfather had been the mayor of the city where I grew up. As a result, my grandparents were always attending some formal affair.) In this particular dream, my grandmother was in a beautiful purple evening gown and matching heels. She looked wonderful. She was healthy and well, not sick as she had been in the nursing home.

In this dream, I was sitting in her kitchen, which looked exactly as it did in my childhood. The cabinetry and tile were white. The sunlight was streaming in through the window and I could smell her fresh-baked goods. Outside of my grandmother's house, the garden was in full bloom and the colors were glorious.

As my grandmother made her way into the kitchen, she saw me sitting at the breakfast table. Sternly she said, "Pull yourself together. I'm fine! Get back to taking care of your boys!" When I woke up, I just had to laugh. This was so like her. After that, I did exactly what she said. I pulled myself together and went on with my life. Was I imagining things? I don't think so. This dream was lucid and realistic. Even after I woke up, I felt my grandmother's presence.

The above experience is called an ADC (after-death communication) dream. In this situation, my grandmother visited me after she had passed over. Such dreams—as with many other DBVs—tend to bring the bereaved a great deal of peace. Years ago, I was working with a woman who had lost her husband. She was devastated by his untimely death. Left with two small children to raise by herself, she was extremely distraught, cried nonstop and was generally overwhelmed with the prospect of living life without her loved one. One day, all of this changed. While meeting for one of our usual therapy sessions, I noticed that—unlike previous sessions—she was now very calm and serene. When I asked her about her change, she said, "He came to me last night. My husband came to me in a dream and it was so real! He told me not to worry about him. He said he was doing fine and then he added that he would always be there to help me with the kids. And, he looked whole, healthy and happy!" This man had died in a violent air crash and the details of recovering his body had been gruesome, to say the least. As she continued discussing this dream, it became obvious that the encounter had been extremely healing for her. ADC researchers have collected numerous accounts of dreams of this nature. Over and over again, the main theme is, "I'm okay, death is not the end and I love you."

DREAMS OF APPROACHING DEATH

As mentioned earlier, dreams about an upcoming death appear throughout literature. Documentation of the dreams of the dying—which include visions of angels, heaven, beautiful cites, crossing over sparkling rivers or deep, lush valleys—are easily found in poetry, fictional works and art. Thumb through the Bible, and you'll find that the angel of death is a theme that prevails in this particular spiritual writing.

Over the last several years, I have collected reports of a number of dreams that related to approaching death. With the definition originally put forth by Osis and Haraldsson, dreams—along with the unusual dream experiences of survivors—are not viewed as DBVs. For the purposes of this book, I will be expanding on the original Osis and Haraldsson DBV definition by including certain dreams of the dying and paranormal dream experiences of surviving family and friends. Like my ancestors, I believe dreams provide a doorway through which our deceased loved ones can communicate with us. Though grief is a real basis for many of our dreams, I also believe some of these dreams may come from an emotional plane of existence that is beyond our present comprehension. Consider the following dream.

On July 23, I had an urge to call my dad, but I didn't. I had not heard from him in a couple of weeks. That night I had the same dream, three times. Each time, I found myself standing at the railroad tracks. Then I would turn left to see the train, just as it hit me. Initially I did feel this dream had something to do with my dad, but at the time, I couldn't quite put my finger on it. Later, I realized the significance of the train. My dad was a longtime railroad employee. I told several people about the dream, but then forgot about it until they reminded me of it later.

My sister was camping that week. My dad did not like camping and didn't go with them. That same Friday night, the twenty-third, she dreamed the phone rang in her camper and my dad was saying, "Your mother (who is deceased) is here. God let her come down and help me because I need her." In her dream, Dad then put her mother on the phone and she said, "Your daddy is about to have a stroke. You need to leave right now and get to his house because he needs you." My sister said her mother's (my step-mother's) voice was as clear as a bell.

The next morning, my sister called Dad at about 9:30. He said he was fine, so she dismissed her worries. An hour later he went out to mow the yard. At 10:30, a neighbor waved at him as he finished the front yard and went around to the back. Evidently, he had mowed two strips of the backyard, turned the mower off, slumped forward and died instantly.

I started calling Dad that afternoon but of course could not reach him. Later on that night (on a Saturday evening), I called my uncle and my brother, who told me to quit worrying. Sunday morning my aunt called. I did not tell her I was looking for my dad. I had decided he had probably gone camping with my sister. She said she had a dream about him the previous night.

My aunt said that in her dream, she was at a restaurant and my dad was there. She then said my dad would turn into her father (my grandfather) and then back to himself again. My aunt added they both looked very young. Because my grandfather had not died that long ago, I said to my aunt, "Since they both looked so young in your dream, we better not find out Daddy has passed on!" Then my aunt continued to tell me about her dream. . . . At this point, I called my dad's church and the neighbor who had seen him mowing the yard the day before had found him dead, in the backyard, still on the mower.

Both women had DBV dreams before the actual death occurred. The aunt had an after-death communication dream about not only the man who passed, but her father. It would appear that the dying man's father-in-law came to offer him a hand in making his way to the next world. Also, isn't it interesting that both men looked young and healthy in this dream?

The woman who shared this account with me had another DBV dream prior to this experience.

I had another experience in 1977. In this dream a very dear friend of mine came to me and told me he was dying. He also told me that everything was fine. I was telephoned the next morning and told he had died at the time I had my dream.

Can those who are leaving us really pay us a visit in our dreams to let us know they are moving on? Here is a dream a woman had about an upcoming death. This account comes from Randles and Hough's book, *The After Life* (1994).

In one case at Wallasey, on Wirral, in 1970, a man and wife had just climbed into bed and turned out the light when they both saw "hovering at (their) side a head, body, but no face. . . ." The woman screamed, but her husband calmed her down assuring her that he could see it too. As soon as they switched the light on, it disappeared.

This incident occurred on a Monday night. On Tuesday the woman dreamed that her grandmother had died. She dismissed this as just a dream, but on Wednesday a caller arrived with a letter for them (her and her husband) which announced her grandmother had indeed passed away, at what appears to have been the same time that they both saw the apparition.

In this particular case, we not only have a dream of a death, but a strange, otherworldly vision the night before. Are the above dream and death of the grandmother just a coincidence?

Let's take a look at another DBV account involving dreams. This one comes from the editor of this book, Christine Belleris. Notice the premonition Christine's dream provided her regarding her father's upcoming death. Was she being prepared ahead of time for his passing?

When I was a freshman in college, my father, Nick, was diagnosed with prostate cancer. The radiation treatments and surgery seemed to have worked, and I was able to enjoy the rest of my college years thinking he was cancer-free.

That same year, however, I had a strange dream. It was so vivid I wrote a poem about it. In the dream, I am standing in front of my house on a barren plain. The sky is orange and purple as you would see it at sunrise. All of a sudden, I see a bright white light up in the sky. It is mesmerizing because it is so intense. The ball of white light then turns into a biplane that is doing loop-de-loops. I realize that the plane is out of control and I can hear the pilot making a strange moaning sound that soon becomes deafening. I know he is going to crash, but there is nothing I can do; my feet are frozen to the ground. I wake up shaking.

Four and a half years later on Christmas Eve, Denver was hit by a big blizzard that dumped two feet of snow on the city. My father woke up early, just as he always did, just before dawn. While looking out the back window, over a barren plain [similar to the plain described in her dream] he said he saw a lone coyote.

A few days after Christmas, he became very ill and we had to take him to the hospital. The cancer was back. He had only days, maybe hours, to live. He had told no one of the disease's reappearance and chose not to go through chemotherapy.

My mother told me he had been dreaming about his deceased family; his mother and father had died when he was in his early twenties (a DBV for her father). No one really thought about what that meant when it was happening.

My father eventually lapsed into a coma. He moaned that same moan I heard in my dream four and a half years earlier. I couldn't get the sound out of my head. That night, a series of unusual circumstances made us miss our ride home and so my mother and I slept at the hospital. Just before dawn, she nudged me awake. My father was dying. I went to his bedside and held his hand.

The head nurse, a stern woman, told me my father was dying and then instructed me not to tell him to stay. I listened to his moaning and saw his eyes, which before had remained fixed and unfocused, follow something across the ceiling in the room. As they shifted all the way to the right, he took his last breath. In that instant, he was just a body, not the father I adored. At that moment, I had an undeniable feeling that he was gone. I looked outside at the morning sky: It was a soft palette of orange and purple as in my dream about the biplane.

After he died, I seemed to feel his presence for a time just behind my left shoulder. I begged him to come see me, to give me a sign that he was there. One night, in the twilight stage just before sleep, I saw his face as clear as day. I woke up with a start. He also appeared to my youngest nephew in a dream. He told Alex, then six years old, to take care of his mommy and let her know that he was okay.

After I had my baby, whom I named Nicholas after my father, I would sometimes feel a breath in my face when I was nursing. It could not possibly have come from the baby.

Recently, I was giving my two-year-old Nicholas a bath. Suddenly he started saying "Hello, hello." Though I couldn't see a thing, it was obvious to me my son was talking to someone in the room. When I asked him who he was saying "hello" to, he said "Grandpa" in Greek. Though he never met my father, he had seen photos of him. I'd like to think it was my father and that he continues to watch over us.

In this account, we have Christine's vivid DBV dream of her father's death, which was to take place four and a half years later. Symbolically, the pilot of a biplane crashes to the plain below. Though her father appears to be past the cancer, Christine's dream is trying to tell her otherwise. As her father's time of passing nears, more pieces of her dream are played out. When her father finally dies, the purple and orange dawn is breaking, just as it did in her dream.

Christine's father also experiences DBVs in the form of dreams about his deceased parents. Also, when he is just about to cross the threshold of death, he experiences the deathbed stare, fixating his vision on a certain part of the environment and appearing to follow a moving image.

Finally, Christine ends her account with several after-death communication experiences. Not only does she feel her father's presence, but when she asks to see him, he appears. Nick comes to his other daughter's son, Christine's nephew and his grandson, in a dream with a message for this child's mother. Several years later, it appears as though Nick paid a visit to his namesake Nicholas, Christine's son, during the child's bath time and to Christine while breast-feeding. These experiences have given Christine and her family a great deal of peace and comfort. Though she continues to miss her beloved father, Christine is comforted in knowing he is just a "breath" away.

The next DBV dream account was initially very confusing for a young woman. As for Christine, not until this woman's father became ill and passed did she understand the meaning of her dream.

I used to have vivid dreams of my dad's funeral . . . what he would wear . . . making all of the arrangements for that day. I never told him of these dreams, but my mom knew about them. The dreams were always the same ones. I could see him lying in his casket and (I knew) how I would feel. I was very calm.

A number of years ago, I was working with a woman in my clinical practice who had experienced a dream just like the aforementioned one. She told me that for years before her husband died, from an accidental overdose of drugs, she had what she called her "coffin dreams." She too would see her loved one in a coffin. Initially, when her dreams began, her husband's drug use was at a minimum and his death was the furthest thing from her conscious mind. Because of this, the dreams were very confusing for her. After he passed, the dreams not only went away, but in retrospect their meaning became very clear. Was her subconscious trying to tell her something or was this a premonition from beyond? In another curious DBV dream, the dreamer envisions reuniting with her deceased loved ones.

The week before my mother's death, we were all remembering my dad and feeling quite sad. Then my mother had a dream that she was in heaven with my dad, her parents and siblings. She was very happy. I tend to think she was able to peek into her future, and that brought her peace.

The narrator of this account told me she and her family had no idea this woman would be dying so soon. Obviously the woman's dream was telling her otherwise. Like Christine's father, did this woman have a DBV visitation from deceased loved ones during her dream? Had they come to assist her in her dying process? The next account may provide some insight.

My mom died in 1995 after being in intensive care for seven weeks. Her sister—who was much younger and, except for high blood pressure, in good health—was devastated by my mom's death. Three months after my mom's death, her sister called me on a Tuesday night and told me that my mom and her older sister (who had also passed) had come to her in a dream and asked her to join them. She said she told them she did not want to. This dream occurred on a Monday night. Thursday night at 11:45 P.M., my aunt died. Strange but true.

This dying woman said "No" to an invitation of assistance offered to her from her deceased loved ones in a DBV dream. Like it or not, several days after this dream she went to join her sisters on the other side. Is there a part of us that knows just when we or our loved ones will pass?

The following DBV dream account involves another

unwanted invitation to the afterlife. Notice the similarities to the previous report.

A week before my father died, he had a dream. He woke up and saw a light in the living room, so he got up to investigate. My father's leg had been amputated five years prior and he used a wheelchair, but in this vision he was whole and walked into the living room. In there were his mother and sister. In the dream they said to him, "You look tired, please come with us." He said, "No, I am not ready yet." They pleaded with him some more, but he was resolute about not going then. He returned to his bed and woke up. This time he tried to get out of bed and found that he needed his chair, because his leg was gone. He went back into the living room and his mother and sister had left. He died seven days later, in his sleep, at home.

Once again, a deceased relative visits in a dream and invites the living to come across. Some researchers believe we are all connected on an unconscious level. Are we? If this is true, does part of us sense when death is near for ourselves or our loved ones? To explore this idea further, let's examine the following DBV dream.

My brother died in June 1998. Before he passed he exhibited no evidence of being ill. He looked just fine! I dreamt of being at his funeral two weeks before he actually died.

How did this woman's unconscious mind know that her brother would soon pass away? Was she receiving a two-week warning to prepare her for his upcoming death, or was this dream just a coincidence? A buddy of mine recently shared a DBV experience that sheds light on this exact issue.

Troy is retired from the space industry and is a religious man. He and I have been meeting weekly with a group of other folks for almost sixteen years. Troy had a very out-spoken mother, and I loved hearing about his experiences with her. She became very ill, and Troy knew that her time was quickly passing. The following DBV dream brought both Troy and his mother a great deal of comfort. Not long after this, she crossed over to the afterlife.

> *Toward the end of January, I was sitting by her bed going through the mail—something I did two or three times a week—when she woke up from a comfortable sleep and told me matter-of-factly that she had been visiting with "Papa." "Papa" was my dad who had died many years earlier. My mother passed a month later.*

Troy told me he never questioned the validity of his mother's dream. As he said to me, "My dad came to see Mom in a dream. I know it for a fact. He was there."

Third-Party Intervention

DBV dreams need not come to a direct relation. Sometimes they appear to anyone connected with an upcoming passing. NDE researcher Melvin Morse presented an interesting DBV dream in his wonderful book, *Closer to the Light* (1993). In the following case, the family wasn't listening, so a DBV message had to be sent through a family pastor.

A five-year-old boy is extremely ill with a brain tumor. Three weeks before he dies, he slips into a coma. During this time, his family is sitting at his bedside twenty-four hours a day praying for his health to return. Because the boy is in a coma, he can't express his desires to his family. As a result, he needs to find another avenue for communication.

The family's pastor came to the hospital at the end of the third week. When he saw the family members he said he had a message for them. The pastor then announced that he had recently had a dream and that in this dream, the boy lying in the bed had come to him. It was "as though he was right there in the room, talking to me face to face," the pastor said. He also shared that the dream had been lifelike and vivid. The pastor then continued by adding that in this dream the boy had announced, "It's my time to die. You must tell my parents to quit praying. I am supposed to go now."

After the pastor was through delivering his message, the parents of the dying boy said one final prayer. Then they told their son they would miss him, but understood his need to go. In essence, the family finally gave the child permission to die. The boy suddenly regained consciousness. He thanked his family for finally letting him go and said he would be dying soon. He died the following day.

If the boy had not been able to come to his pastor in a dream, who knows how long the parents would have continued praying for their poor child. I have already told my husband, "Honey, if I look like I'm just hanging on by a thread, and everything that can possibly be done has been done, please don't pray for me! And for heaven's sake, if it isn't necessary, don't prolong my life!"

For many of us, determining when we should let go is difficult, perhaps because of our unwillingness to trust our intuition. Ignoring our intuition can also interfere with our ability to psychically hear, see and feel the loving touches of passing dear ones. Because we are not trusting this "sixth sense" we risk missing those messages the dying wish to pass on to us.

CONNECTIONS AT THE MOMENT OF DEATH

As discussed in the first chapter, I was awakened early one morning by a strong sense that my mother had died. Though the skeptic can blame such experiences on the haze of sleep, an overactive imagination and coincidence, I disagree with such conclusions. With DBV experiences, I strongly believe that more is going on than the black-and-white interpretations of science. Read the following account and notice how similar it is to the DBV with my mother.

I woke up with my heart pounding at 4:15 on the morning of November 20, 1997. I couldn't go back to sleep and was very restless and agitated. Two hours later, my uncle called to tell me Daddy had died at about 4:15. He went very peacefully and quietly. Later, I found out that my grandmother (my mother's mother) had awakened suddenly at around four that morning. The nurses at the nursing home called to tell me she was very agitated. When I was back in Florida for the funeral, the next-door neighbor said she and her husband were awakened at 4:15 that morning. Could Dad have been announcing his departure like everything else he did in life—great fanfare and hoopla? Sure sounds like it!

In the above account, the daughter, mother and neighbors all awake at the moment of the father's death. If you will remember, at the instant of my mother's passing, two of my mother's dear friends and I all woke up from a deep sleep and knew she was gone. We all felt her leave this life.

In my clinical psychotherapy practice, the surviving spouses of a departed individual often talk about feeling as though a piece of them is suddenly gone. When sharing about this feeling, the most common word used is "loss." Notice how empty the following narrator felt *before* discovering her father had just died of heart failure and pneumonia.

The night of his death, I had an overwhelming feeling of loss. I was incredibly sad, but I put this down to the fact that it was the anniversary of my mother's funeral a week earlier. People who knew me and saw me that evening commented on the fact that something was bothering me and that they could sense the sadness. They also thought it was about my mother. But you know, I am not sure that was it. I felt a huge loss and felt so very alone. It was the worst night I have had in a long time. This may sound crazy, but I think I was connected to my dad in some way, and I knew his time was near. I feel that on that night, I must have somehow known, or felt him dying, before I knew he had died. I have never hurt so much in an evening for what I thought was no reason.

In this case, this daughter almost seemed to be experiencing her father's death process.

Many years ago, my husband and I were in Taos, New Mexico, attending a workshop. One evening, I felt extremely uneasy and very agitated. My mood was foul and I couldn't put my finger on exactly what was happening. All I knew was that I felt very disturbed. The following morning, my mother-in-law called to tell us Uncle Bill had died. After I heard this, my agitated mood the night before made a great deal of sense. Like the narrator in the previous account, I was aware on some level that Uncle Bill was moving on.

This sense of being "touched" by a departing loved one has been with us throughout history. For some strange reason, those near death often announce their exit from this life in the middle of the night. The following 1884 account comes from a Time-Life book titled *Phantom Encounters* (1998). In this DBV example, a young groom-to-be receives more than a light tap on the shoulder.

Professor Romanes recorded a curious incident involving a handsome young Englishman named Griffiths, who was about to marry a lovely French girl. Chaperoned by their mothers, the betrothed pair had just spent a pleasant holi-day in Italy and the south of France and were on their way home, the Griffiths to London and the French girl with her mother to Paris. One night before crossing the channel to England, young Griffiths was awakened from a heavy sleep to hear the voice of his fiancée pleading with him in French to come instantly to her in Paris.

Griffiths then saw his betrothed coming toward him and felt her reach out to grasp his arm in her hand. An awful fright took hold of him, and the Englishman rushed to his mother's room. As might be expected, she calmly reassured him that everything was all right, and he returned to his bed. He fell asleep but was soon conscious of an intense pain on his arm. Rolling up his nightshirt sleeve, he found an ugly red spot and a rising blister where his love had touched him.

Next morning, Griffiths visited a doctor, who told him that he had suffered a severe burn. But that seemed impos-sible, and doubly so because the doctor could not find the slightest indication of fire or corrosive chemical on the sleeve of the nightshirt.

Later that day, a telegram arrived from Paris bringing
news of his fiancée's sudden death, following an illness of
only a few hours. Some time after that, Griffiths learned
that as she lay dying she had called out for him in the very
words he had heard in his bedroom.

With the above encounter, the Englishman is awakened
by his beloved's voice as she lays dying miles away. When I
initially saw this particular DBV, I read it to my husband and
said, "If you die before I do, come give me one final hug, but
please, let it be a gentle hug!" Feeling or sensing the departure of the dying as they pass can be an overwhelming sensation. If we do not have others to share this encounter with,
we are often left wondering, "Am I dreaming?"

When I was with Raymond Moody several years ago, a
woman from New York made contact with her deceased
husband and, in doing so, experienced his death process.
The following narrator had a similar experience, but hers
took place as her mother was passing.

I was working part time at night at a twenty-four-hour
convenience store. My hours were usually from 7 P.M. until
1 to 2 A.M. On June 15, I arrived home at a little after 1 A.M.
I wasn't home long when suddenly I was buffeted by emo-
tions, chest pains and weakness. The chest pains started
first, then the tears. I was driven to the floor and was
rocking back and forth. I also had certain thoughts going
through my mind, but somehow I knew they were not my

own, just as I knew that what was happening to me really wasn't happening to me. I didn't know exactly what was happening, but at the same time, I didn't feel any fear for myself. I had no control over any of this but could do nothing about it. All I could do was experience it.

The thoughts that kept running through my mind were, I am not ready, I can't die like this. Oh, please, please not like this. . . . My kids, what about the kids? *The tears and the emotions were overpowering. A short time later, it all of a sudden stopped, like someone had thrown a switch. I felt like I had been drained of every bit of strength I had, and I was so tired that all I could do was wonder what the hell had just happened to me. After this, I made my way to bed. The next day I told my husband about what had happened, and he was as confused about it as I was.*

On June 17 at 5 P.M., a friend of my mom's called. Mom lived about thirty miles away. The friend told me he hadn't heard from my mother and said because she didn't answer the phone, he went to her apartment and broke down her front door. He found her sitting on the floor, leaning against a hassock. She had passed on. I freaked, of course, and the police requested that I come by her apartment. By the time I arrived, the coroner had come and gone. I was told her time of passing was between 1 and 3 A.M. on the same day I had my overwhelming emotional and physical experience.

I felt like I had gotten a double shock, not just that she had passed, but that my experience was related to this. I had felt her passing as she went. All of it, the chest pains (her death was the result of a heart attack), her emotions, her tears and thoughts.

I had even been driven to sit on the floor like she had.

For a long time, I felt that if I had known my experience was really about what was happening to her, I could have called an ambulance for her or helped her in some way. But, the reality of it is, nothing would have changed. My experience was not about saving her. It was about sharing it with her. I don't know why this happened and I doubt I ever will know, until I can ask her. She does visit now and again in after-death communications, but it's usually to help me with my brother and sister when they need it.

When I first shared this account with a few of my more open-minded friends, they looked at me as if I was short a marble or two and then said, "Yeah, right, Carla." Then I shared with them the following DBV, presented in *Phantom Encounters*.

In an incident recorded by Louisa Rhine, a woman in California awoke at 4:00 A.M. one day in 1955, convinced that she was dying. She had the sensation of blood pouring from her head as if from a wound and found herself gasping and choking. As her husband helped her drink some water, the woman distinctly heard the voice of her son call, "Oh, Mama, help me." Two days later the doctor assured her that nothing was physically wrong with her, (but) the woman learned that her son, a soldier stationed in Germany, had received a fatal gunshot wound to the head at exactly the time of her attack.

Are we all psychically connected? Could the intense bond that we have with our loved ones be so strong that we are able to feel their emotional or physical pain as they pass? Do long-deceased friends reach out to the dying in dreams to help them cross over into an afterlife existence? Can the dying walk into the dreams of the living in order to take care of unfinished business? Do we have a sixth sense that alerts us when death is near? These questions and others deserve to be researched by the scientific community. Hopefully—some day—accounts such as those presented in this chapter will not just been seen as strange ghost stories. Perhaps society will recognize that these messages from beyond truly are postcards from departing loved ones. With proper investigation we just might realize we are never left alone, in life or in death.

Chapter 7

The Many Consequences of Spiritual Encounters

"Take away these pillows — I shall need them no more."

Parting words of Lewis Carroll

Wouldn't it be great if the scientific community was really interested in the numerous spiritual encounters so many of us seem to have? Think how healing it would be for both the dying and their family members to routinely hear from hospital personnel that DBVs were normal! Imagine the relief those at the bedside would feel upon hearing that the deathbed stare was not the by-product of a miswired brain, but instead the result of a spiritual encounter with the other side. Such healing would occur!

I have often thought, *If only there had been a modern-day book on DBVs for me to read when my mother died. Wouldn't it have been great if DBVs were seen as normal?*

When I first experienced the deathbed vision with my mother, I was only sixteen and afraid to tell a soul. My fear was that I would have to listen to comments like, "Have you lost your mind? Get a grip! Stop talking nonsense!" How wonderful instead it would have been to hear, "You felt your mother's presence before she left! That's great! Don't you know that is normal? What a blessing! Yes, love continues and never dies."

Thinking back on the trauma and confusion of my mother's death, I often think of how often I tried to forget my own DBV. In an attempt to bury the whole experience, I started drinking alcohol. No one was willing to talk to me about death and dying. Discussions of the afterlife were definitely out. As a teenager, emotionally I was incapable of understanding my mother's death or the DBV. It all seemed so overwhelming. The alcohol blunted the constant and intense pain.

To this day, I can still visualize myself as a young girl, dressed in a beautiful green dress I had made. At the cemetery, I had floated from one person to the next, thanking them for attending my mother's funeral. My blue-haired grandmother had given my sisters and me tranquilizers. She had even put a few of these little white pills in my grandfather's peanut butter sandwich. We were all zoned out at the funeral, and I only remember crying once. I'm amazed I remember anything from that day.

Once the funeral was over, I was totally alone. Only the wine I drank nightly eased my agony. With the help of open-minded adults, my DBV could have been used to assist me with my grieving. Discussions of death, dying and spiritual afterlife encounters would have mended my broken heart. Instead, I was confronted with silence. As a result, I tucked my precious DBV away and turned to the wine bottle, which almost killed me.

My reason for revisiting this period in my life is simple. Because this topic is still snickered at by major newspapers, magazines and scientific journals, many DBV experiencers continue to hide and even suffer in grief. This open discounting of spiritual encounters perpetuates disbelief. Tabloids and television talk shows continue to exploit spiritual encounters with a great deal of sensationalism. For the unaware public at large, such actions denigrate the importance of DBVs and related phenomena.

The majority of the scientific community and media have made it difficult for people who have deathbed visions, after-death communications or near-death experiences to feel comfortable sharing them with others. When our spiritual encounters are minimized by the general press and the scientific community, people who have not had these experiences are reluctant to accept otherworldly contact and spiritual encounters. After reading the following account, you should see what I mean.

My cousin had a heart attack at fourteen and was clini-
cally dead for some time. After he was revived, he was able
to see spirits. I suspect this was due to his near-death expe-
rience. Anyway, he came to visit my grandpa, who was still
at home before being admitted to the hospital for an illness.
My aunt was at my grandpa's bedside, and my cousin asked
her, "Has anything strange happened yet?" His mother
asked why. He responded, "Well, with all of these spirits
here, I'm surprised nothing has happened."

He then told me that he saw my deceased grandmother
rubbing Grandpa's leg, while other deceased relatives stood
by the bedside. Upon hearing this, his mother (my aunt)
freaked out and ran out of the room.

Though the cousins had talked about such experiences, the poor mother in this case was frightened out of her wits by the visions. Such experiences were obviously not commonplace for her. Fear of the unknown was overwhelming. In our culture, where children are sheltered from death, normal occurrences during the dying process end up being unnerving for the unaware survivor.

My husband's first DBV encounter at his father's deathbed was a spiritual experience for him. Unfortunately, he felt he had to be very careful about whom he shared it with. His ADC encounter, where he saw his father in physical form sitting in our downstairs parlor after he had died, was very comforting for him. But, once again, he felt as though he couldn't openly talk about it. Michael wasn't frightened of either of these experiences. Unlike most people in society, he had been exposed to this type of phenomena before his father passed.

Though the DBV and the ADC affected him positively, for several years Michael would not speak to certain family, friends or professional peers of his experience. "Yeah, that is all I need. I can hear it now, 'Local shrink sees dead father. Yes, he needs medication, and the dose should be tripled!' People just don't get this stuff." My husband is right. Most people tend to see this sort of activity as abnormal.

CONSISTENCY OF PURPOSE

Much debate surrounds the origins of deathbed visions. Science uses a number of theories to explain away such visions, such as mental illness, excessive grief, wishful thinking, hysteria, hallucinations or an overactive imagination. Recently, one physician friend of mine asked, "Couldn't DBVs just be the result of the brain dying?" Instead of arguing with him, I answered him with another question, one that was put to me in recent e-mail correspondence from a woman named Beverly. After you read her words, ask yourself the following question: "Is the dying brain theory just another simplistic catch-all answer to the mysterious DBV inquiry?"

[A]s you continue to investigate deathbed visions, would you look for an answer to this question of mine? There has been a lot of debate about these visions. Most of the debate rotates around how people frequently see their loved ones who have already passed on as they themselves are dying. The rational, scientific explanation to this has been that while dying, the brain is randomly firing off images from its memory banks. If it is random firing of the brain, why are the visions not of relatives and friends who are still alive? Or people they have seen on TV or in the grocery store? These folks would be in the memory bank as well.

Beverly has made an important point. If DBVs are just the result of a dying brain, oxygen deprivation, neurosis or chemical imbalances, why are most of the visions of people who are deceased? Why do these visions typically involve not just visions, but visitations from the other side? If DBVs were hallucinations or the result of random firing of brain synapses, why are the themes of these visions so consistent with one another? Hallucinations from one person to the next are not this consistent. The by-product of random firings of the brain produces chaotic visions, not consistent encounters with deceased relatives.

Finally, I have one more question for the scientists. How come the task of these DBV messengers consistently appears to involve providing comfort to the dying and validation of an afterlife existence? As a practicing clinical therapist, with over twenty years experience in the mental health field, I have yet to see a series of consistent task-oriented themes within the hallucinations of a group of hallucinating individuals. With DBVs, the consistent goal of the messenger is to assist with the dying process.

Research (Osis and Haraldsson [1977]) shows that during deathbed visions, the deceased relatives, friends, angels or other religious beings usually appear for the specific purpose of escorting a loved one to the other side. If such visions were only the result of the chemistry of a dying brain, why would these encounters have such a defined purpose? Are we biologically programmed to have such visions before we pass? I don't think so. Finally, why do living relatives and friends have DBVs that have characteristics similar to the dying? The dying-brain or random-firing-of-the-brain theories just don't work in these cases. To see what I mean, read the following DBV account, which comes from a physician friend of mine.

My father died very unexpectedly. Up to that point, he had been fine and nobody would have thought it was his time to pass. Just before he died, my aunt (his sister) had a very strange dream. She dreamed that the family was all together. Everybody was there, including her son who had been killed in Vietnam. In the dream, everyone in the family knew the son was dead, but they all acted as if it were perfectly normal for him to be at this gathering. After much visiting, one of the relatives finally asked this Vietnam soldier, "Why are you here?" He answered, "I'm here to take someone back with me." Very shortly after that, my dad died.

Wishful Thinking?

Some people in the scientific community have also said that deathbed visions of the dying are a by-product of wishful thinking. According to this particular theory, when death nears, the dying have such visions because of a strong desire for an afterlife. How does such a hypothesis explain the following deathbed vision? This case—one of my favorites—was also given to me by a physician.

My grandmother was great and we all loved her so much. She was such a character. The family knew she was passing, so we all gathered around her deathbed. We were visiting with each other while my grandmother laid quietly in her bed. Suddenly, without warning, she sat up and said, "Now why on earth is he here?" We all stopped talking and immediately focused our attention on her. "Over there," she said. "It's your grandfather!" My grandfather had been deceased for some time. "I didn't want him to come! I didn't expect him to come! I wanted (names of other deceased family members, including her son) to come see me when I got to this point." My grandmother was most serious about this.

Upon hearing her, the family sitting around her bed burst out laughing. It was hysterical, but in keeping with my grandmother. Then she added, "Well, I always did wonder where he had gone off to. Now I guess I know!" Shortly after this she passed.

If deathbed visions were only a product of wishful thinking, why was this woman not visited by those deceased relatives *she* had expected to see? Such an account gives us all something to contemplate.

SIGHTING THE UNKNOWN DEAD

The scientific community also has a great deal of difficulty explaining a very specific type of deathbed vision: when the dying have visions of people they believe are still living. In actuality, the loved ones seen in these DBVs are actually deceased. The dying individual just isn't aware that these particular individuals have passed.

Barrett presented the following case in his research (1926). This particular account was originally given to the American Society for Psychical Research by the Reverend J. A. McDonald. The reverend heard this account from Miss Ogle, the dying man's sister.

My brother, John Alkin Ogel, died in Leeds, July 17, 1879. About an hour before he expired, he saw his brother . . . who

had died about sixteen years before . . . and John, looking up
with a fixed interest, said, "Joe! Joe!" and immediately after
exclaimed with ardent surprise, "George Hanley!" My
mother, who had come from Melbourne, a distance of about
forty miles, where George Hanley resided, was astonished at
this, and said, "How strange he should see George Hanley;
he died only ten days ago." Then, turning to my sister-in-
law, she asked if anybody had told John of George Hanley's
death; she (the sister-in-law) said, "No one." My mother was
the only person present who was aware of the fact. I was
present and witnessed this.

Barrett then states that Miss Ogle received inquires
about her brother's visions and to these she answered:

J. A. Ogle was neither delirious nor unconscious when he
uttered the words recorded. George Hanley was an
acquaintance of John A. Ogle, not a particularly familiar
friend. The death of Hanley was not mentioned in his hear-
ing (he never heard about it).

How did this dying man know his acquaintance had
passed on? In this account, we hear that he was visited by
his brother, Joe. John knew Joe was deceased, but he didn't
know George had died.

Another account taken from Barrett's collection once
again involves a visitation not just from one deceased
friend, but several. In this example as above, the dying individual is completely unaware that these visitors are all dead.

My uncle, M. Paul Durocq, left Paris in 1893 for a trip to America with my aunt and other members of the family. While they were at Venezuela my uncle was seized with yellow fever, and he died at Caracas on the 24th of June 1894.

Just before his death, and while surrounded by all of his family, he had a prolonged delirium, during which he called out the names of certain friends left in France, and whom he seemed to see. "Well, well, you too . . . , and you . . . , and you as well!"

Although struck by this incident, nobody attached any extraordinary importance to these words at the time they were uttered, but they acquired later an exceptional importance when the family found, on their return to Paris, the funeral invitation cards of the persons named by my uncle before his death, and who had died before him.

The children of the dying uncle, Germaine and Maurice, added the following to the above account.

Germaine stated,

You asked me details of the death of my poor father. I well remember him laying dying, though it is many years ago. The thing which probably interests you is that he told us of having seen some persons in heaven and of having spoken to them at some length. We were much astonished on returning to France to find the funeral cards of those same persons whom he had seen when dying. Maurice, who was older than I was, could give you more details on the subject.

Maurice added,

Concerning what you ask me with regard to the death of my father, which occurred a good many years ago, I recall that a few moments before his death my father called the name of one of his old companions—M. Etcheverry—with whom he had not kept up any connection, even by correspondence, for a long time past, crying out, "Ah! You too," or some similar phrase. It was only on returning home to Paris that we found the funeral card of this gentleman.

In another of Barrett's accounts, a dying girl in Brazil has a visitation from her brother. Her father, who is at her bedside, believes the brother is still alive.

A few hours before her death, the patient said to her father that she saw near her bed several members of the family, all deceased some years previously. The father attributed this declaration in extremis to a state of delirium, but Adamina insisted with renewed force, and among the invisible "visitors" named her own brother, Alfredo, who was employed at the time at a distance of 423 kilometers, on the lighthouse of the port of Sisal.

The father was more and more convinced of the imaginary nature of these visions, well knowing that his son Alfredo was in perfect health, for a few days previous he had sent the best possible news of himself.

Adamina died that same evening, and the next morning her father received a telegram informing him of the death of the young Alfredo. A comparison of times showed that the dying girl was still living at the time of the death of her brother.

Barrett has several other accounts of this nature, all of which serve to reinforce this aspect of the DBV phenomena.

More recent accounts of this phenomena also exist. The following deathbed vision comes from Natalie Kalmus, best known for her contribution to the development of the Technicolor process. R. DeWitt Miller in his book, *You DO Take It with You* (1955), shares what Natalie's sister Eleanor had to say as she passed.

I sat on her bed and took her hand. It was on fire. Then Eleanor seemed to rise up in bed, almost to a sitting position.

"Natalie," she said, "there are so many of them. There's Fred and Ruth—what's she doing here?"

An electric shock went through me. She had said Ruth! Ruth was her cousin, who had died suddenly a week before. But I knew that Eleanor had not been told of the sudden death. . . . I felt on the verge of some wonderful, almost frightening knowledge. . . .

Her voice was surprisingly clear. "It's so confusing. There are so many of them!" Suddenly her arms stretched out happily. "I am going up with them," she murmured.

Yes, Eleanor passed on.

The following narrative comes to us from Great Britain.

In *The After-Death Experience* (1987), Ian Wilson provides the reader with the following personal account.

> *In 1968 Mrs. Janet T., wife of a Bristol accountant, gave birth to a baby daughter Jane, who sadly died of pneumonia two days later. Shortly after, some one hundred miles away in the village of Llangernyw near Abergele in North Wales, Janet's ninety-six-year-old grandmother, Mrs. Jane Charles, lay dying, attended by Janet's father, Mr. Geoffrey Charles, a newspaper reporter. . . . Mr. Charles had carefully avoided telling his mother that Janet had lost her baby, not least because the infant had quite specifically been given the Christian name Jane in honor of her great-grandmother.*
>
> *So he had no idea of the bombshell that was about to strike when . . . Mrs. Charles began to talk to apparent unseen visitors. Totally clearheaded, she first remarked on a woman who seemed to bother her. Then . . . she became "calm and happy." It was all right, she announced; she "knew what it was all about now." She very contentedly told her son that she had seen his father, her husband John, who had died in 1942. Then, with a puzzled expression, she remarked that the only thing she could not understand was that John (her deceased husband) had a baby with him. She said about this very emphatically:*
>
> *"It's one of our family. It's Janet's poor baby. Never mind, she'll get over it."*
>
> *Hard-bitten journalist though he was, Geoffrey Charles was dumbfounded and choking with emotion when he later telephoned the news to Janet. Mrs. Charles's dying*

prediction came true; for although initially shattered, Janet did get over it, and now has a near grown-up son and daughter.

The author goes on to say that he knew Janet personally and knows for a fact that neither she nor her father had ever read any of the work of the deathbed vision researchers Barrett, Osis or Kübler-Ross. Yet, according to this account, not only does it appear as though the grandparents will survive death, but the baby is already with the grandfather.

I recently received a deathbed vision report from a woman who was with her father when he passed. Note the similarities to the previous accounts.

While my father had been confined to his bed, my brother suddenly passed away. His death was most unexpected and very premature. As a family, we elected to withhold this information from my father for as long as we could.

In less than a week's time of my brother's passing, my father said to us, "I used to have three children, now I only have two." There was absolutely no way he could have known my brother had died. Furthermore, prior to his death, my brother never visited my father more than once a week at the most.

When we asked him why he had said this, he just looked at us as if we were all nuts. Later that week, he finally told us he had seen my brother in a visitation. Along with this, my father made several references to receiving messages from my mother. She has been deceased for fifteen years. It is important for you to know that my father's mind when awake had never been sharper. I truly believe that there is no doubt he had a foot in both worlds.

Fortunately, this dying man had a family who was receptive to his visions. Though they tried to keep his son's death from him, the dying father knew just the same.

Protecting the Survivors

When publicly discussing deathbed vision phenomena, I am often asked, "Why do only some people have such visions? When my relatives and friends were passing, they never reported experiences like that." The following letter I received in 1998 provided an excellent answer to this question.

A friend of mine had a grandfather who was dying in the hospital. The grandfather mentioned to my friend that he had seen a "little man" on his bedside table. The grandfather wanted to know who he was. He also wanted to know where the "staircase in the corner of the room" went up to. In his room, there was no physical staircase. The family did not even consider that this might be a deathbed vision. Instead, they decided the grandfather was just losing his mind.

After hearing this from my friend I thought, These aren't

hallucinations, but visions sent and designed to ease this man's death transition. *Many of the experiences the dying have are discounted by friends, relatives and even hospital personnel. They are viewed as delusions or meaningless experiences and are therefore not investigated.*

Perhaps many dying people refrain from discussing these visions for fear of frightening their loved ones.

I believe that many dying people experience these visions and visitations but do not talk openly about them because of the fear of being labeled "crazy."

In working with the dying, I have also noticed they are often very concerned with how their loved ones will take their passing and may choose to avoid sharing about certain aspects of their dying process. Seeing the distress of loved ones would naturally make it more difficult for some of the dying to share their DBVs.

Where Do We Go from Here?

For thousands of years, descriptive metaphors have been used to depict the course death takes. The man in the previous case saw a stairway leading up to who knows where. We have all heard about the "valley of death," the flight of the spirit to the "Happy Hunting Ground," the "veil of death," being at death's door, a stairway to heaven, travel through a tunnel to a brilliant white light, Jacob's ladder to heaven, entry into "cities of light," "knocking on heaven's door," streets paved in gold, a light at the end of the tunnel and so forth. In paintings on the walls of Egyptian tombs, one can even see the dead being ferried across the River Styx.

Where do these images come from? Moody (1975) and Ring (1980 and 1984) have both collected accounts of heavenly landscapes in the afterlife from those who have had near-death experiences. According to an article in the *Toronto Star* (1977), Arthur Sanders went through a near-death experience after being shot in the abdomen with a shotgun at point-blank range. Pronounced dead on arrival at a hospital, he was resuscitated. During a five-hour operation, Mr. Sanders "died" once more, but was brought back to life by his doctors. While this man was clinically dead, he was able to get a glimpse of what he referred to as "the other world." Here is his account.

I never felt so happy in my entire life. During the time that . . . I died . . . I had an experience that has completely transformed my life. I suddenly felt myself floating up away from my body. I seemed to be out in an open landscape of beautiful scenery which was glittering with an incredible, brilliant golden light. There was a clean, blue sky above me and I seemed to be . . . led on by a kind of shining mist that hovered near. I felt such a sense of joy and exhilaration as I had never known. . . . This sense of utter happiness has not left me. . . . One thing I'm certain of and would like to share with everybody—I'll never, never be afraid of death again. It was quite incredible. . . . What happened . . . has changed my whole way of thinking. . . . The Twenty-third Psalm is my favorite now. You know how it says, "Yea, though I walk through the valley of the shadow of death, I will fear no evil"? Well, that's taken on tremendous meaning. . . . I know it is true. There is no evil to fear because we are going to a far, far better place.

Other near-death experiencers have described encountering learning centers or places of knowledge in the afterlife. Once revived from a close encounter with death, individuals who have left their bodies and visited these centers of learning often describe them as luminous structures, containing all knowledge. From his book, *Heading Toward Omega*, Ring (1984) shares the NDE of a woman who was prevented from entering one of these cities of knowledge. As she gave her account to him, she is said to have wept.

I could hear languages, all languages. Languages that I had never heard before and I could understand them. I wanted to be allowed to go on. I knew there was much more there and I wanted to be able to experience it, to see it. . . . There was the knowledge that was beyond anything that I could possibly try to describe to you. I began to realize that I was going to have to leave and I didn't want to leave.

For many near-death experiencers, the impact of these adventures changes them forever. As Neiman and Goldman (1994) documented in their book, *Afterlife,* after policeman Joe Geraci died and came back, he couldn't talk about his NDE for six months. The experience had been just too overwhelming.

> *It was such an emotional, beautiful, swelling feeling inside that every time I tried to express it, I think I would just explode, you know; I would break down and cry. And she (his wife) for the longest time couldn't figure out what was wrong with me.*

If spiritual encounters were discussed openly, without ridicule or shame, maybe this policeman would not have felt the need to keep this incredible experience to himself. Society dictates what is acceptable conversation. As it stands now, topics involving unusual spiritual phenomena are still looked upon by society with much distrust.

* * *

When I have had afterlife encounters, they have been emotionally moving, incredibly overwhelming, indescribable, life-altering and enlightening. Because these experiences are so positively powerful and different from my normal, everyday existence, I have wanted to reach out and share them with friends, family and peers. I especially want to open up and talk about my DBVs and ADCs if the person I am with is phobic about death or has recently experienced a loss. Though my intentions are always pure, the responses I have received have ranged from total acceptance to, "Are you out of your mind?" Most responses have been of the latter variety.

Time and time again, my joy in relating DBVs or ADCs has been dashed by someone who wants to question not only my reality, but often my sanity! Can I blame those who don't believe me? No, not really. If they have not had encounters of their own, or been exposed to any narrations of DBV, NDE or ADC experiences, my spiritual adventures probably sound like nothing more than fanciful fairy tales.

Hopefully, more and more of us will come forward and openly talk about what we have learned with regard to life after death. Many famous present-day mediums have taken this risk and now regularly appear in the media. This is a beginning, but such experiences will only be seen as normal if a larger number of us—the general public—are willing to open up and share.

Chapter 8

A Journey to the Beyond

"I've never felt better."

Parting words of Douglas Fairbanks

About a decade ago, my husband and I decided to have our wills drawn up. We called an estate lawyer, told him what we wanted to do and he took care of the rest. A week later, our lawyer called us to say, "Can you come by my office sometime today? I need your John Hancocks on these things." After deciding on a time to meet, I hung up the phone and then rode my bike downtown to his office.

When I travel my hometown by bike, I often come across people I know. Though the island attracts many tourists, the locals living permanently in the area are very familiar with one another. As I chained my trusty blue steed to an antique horse hitching post, an acquaintance honked her car horn and waved. She stopped her auto right there in the middle of the street and we started to visit.

"Where are you headed?" she asked as she turned down her radio.

"I'm meeting Michael at our lawyer's office. We need to sign our wills," I replied.

Upon hearing this she appeared confused. "A will!" she exclaimed. "Are you sick? Is Michael all right? Why on earth do you need a will?"

Somewhat surprised by her extreme reaction, I responded, "Nothing is physically wrong with us. We just decided to do our will in case something should happen to us."

My fellow islander looked very uneasy. "What's going to happen to you? You are still young." She paused and then said, "Do you really think you need a will?"

This woman was clearly uncomfortable with this particular line of conversation. Feeling awkward, I decided to try to clarify my desire for a will. "I'm hitting middle age and I have two children. I'm not saying I plan on making my big exit any time soon, but I do want to be prepared." The look on her face immediately told me I had stepped in it again.

"Middle-aged? What are you talking about? I'm older than you are and I don't consider myself middle-aged."

I wasn't going to respond. Instead I just patted her on

the shoulder and prepared to leave. As I turned my bike in the direction of the lawyer's office, I heard, "I guess someday I will have to get a will drawn up, but not anytime soon." I realized that this fifty-something-year-old woman just might be uncomfortable with the idea of dying. Practical preparations for her inevitable passage were far from important to her.

Having married into a family that generally enjoys a long life expectancy, I've been interested to watch the older members of my husband's clan take care of the business of death. Unlike many of the elders on my side of the family, my older in-laws perceive aging and dying as a normal occurrence. All their wills are completed and they have had their cemetery plots picked out for some time. At the family plot, a tombstone engraved with all of the family last names is already standing. The family even has a designated funeral director.

On my side of the family, few older relatives ever made preparations. As a matter of fact, any discussion of death continues to be seen as "morbid" and "depressing." When I asked my eighty-something-year-old grandfather if he had written up his will, the topic of conversation quickly changed. Because my grandmother had such a difficult time with death, she rarely attended funerals. We live in a society that is phobic about death, and sadly this fright is deeply rooted in my own family.

Preparations

In researching DBVs, I have noticed that the dying often know they will shortly be going on some sort of a trip. These soon-to-be departing souls may not be consciously aware of exactly where they will be traveling, but they have a strong sense they are going somewhere. Because they recognize the imminence of this voyage, they often try to prepare.

Dying people who start talking about the arrangements they need to make for their journey to the hereafter are often discouraged from the topic. Family, friends, clergy and even medical personnel will quickly squelch such conversation. Even if the dying appear to have "one foot in the grave," they are often told, "Oh! You will come through this! We know you can do it! Keep a positive attitude!"

Friends or relatives of the dying may try to scold, guilt-trip or chastise the soon-to-be-departing with statements like, "You are not going to be dying soon. Stop talking like that. Take the word *death* right out of your vocabulary! You can't go! How will we survive without you?" With such statements from surviving loved ones, the dying openly recognize the uselessness of conversing about unfinished business, the necessity of a will or preparations for their funeral. When they are told to "stop talking about such morbid things," the dying tend to do just that—often with unfortunate consequences for the survivors.

Michael's father picked his date of departure. My mother waited to die until after my sixteenth birthday. Michael's grandfather didn't make his big exit until after his ninety-seventh birthday. All these people knew they were passing but chose to stick around just long enough to fulfill certain obligations. New York City hospitals reported a highly disproportionate incidence of death in January 2000, and officials surmised that people just wanted to hang on to see the year 2000 arrive.

In days gone by, the entire family was commonly involved in the dying process of a loved one. The individual laying in the deathbed seemed more in control of his or her course of departure. DBVs were shared with family members, loose ends were tied up and good-byes were said. Many of the dying had warnings about their upcoming death, making immediate preparation all the more important. In knowing that her own hour of passing was near, my own mother picked out the music she wanted to be played at her funeral.

Some people who were to die soon even took certain steps to ease the impact of their departure on their loved ones. In 1808 a woman had a very unusual dream about a dear friend of hers who had recently died. In this dream, the departed friend told the surviving woman she would visit her in the future. The deceased woman added that she would visit her friend twenty-four hours before her death.

In March 1864 the surviving woman received a warning from her deceased friend that death is near. Here is the rest of her story, taken from *Proceedings of the Society for Psychical Research* (1899):

> *She told her (her grandson's wife) that Mrs. Carleton (the friend who died years ago) had at last, after an interval of fifty-six years, come to speak to her of her death, which was imminent, and that she would die the morning of the next day, at that same hour. She added that she had, as a precaution, taken a bath to make unnecessary the washing of her dead body. She then began to sink, little by little, and died the morning of March 4th, at the time she had specified. . . .*
>
> *My mother had always told me that she would again see Mrs. Carleton just before her death.*
>
> *Thomas James Norris (the dying woman's son)*
> *Dalkey, Ireland*

The dying woman's physician, Dr. Richard John Lyon from Dublin, Ireland, had this to say about this case.

> *The late Mrs. Doras Norris had told me several times that Mrs. Elisa Carleton had appeared to her in a dream, and had promised to appear to her one last time, twenty-four hours before her death. The night that preceded her death she announced that the warning for which she had waited fifty-six years had been given her, and that she would die the following night, a thing that happened.*

According to the initial report, Mrs. Norris appeared to be in good health when she announced her upcoming death.

Here is another DBV account from Sir Barrett's collection of visions. It is a wonderful example of how the dying will pick their time to move from this world to the next:

In 1862 Dr. Ormsby was acting as assistant surgeon to the 18th Illinois Volunteers; the regiment having gone forward to attack Fort Henry, he was left behind in charge of the sick. Among these was a young man called Albert Adams, a sergeant-major, in whom the doctor seems to have been specially interested. He removed him from the hospital and took him into a private house. The adjoining apartment to that occupied by the patient was divided from his room only by a thin partition; this other room was occupied by the doctor's wife.

The man was dying and all the afternoon he could only speak in whispers; his father was sent for and at 11 P.M. Sergeant Adams to all appearance died. Dr. Ormsby, who was at the time standing beside the father by the bed, states that thinking the bereaved man might faint in keenness of his grief, he led him away to a chair in the back part of the room, and himself returned to the bedside, intending to close the eyes of Adams, who he thought had expired.

Dr. Ormsby then states, "As I reached the bedside the supposed dead man looked suddenly up in my face, and said,

'Doctor, what day is it?' I told him the day of the month, and he answered, 'That is the day I died.' His father had sprung to the bedside, and Adams turning his eyes on him said, 'Father, our boys (the fighting army) have taken Fort Henry, and Charlie (his brother involved in the fight) isn't hurt. I've seen mother and the children and they are well.'

"He then gave comprehensive directions regarding his funeral. . . . He then turned toward me and again said, 'Doctor, what day is it?' and I answered him as before. He again repeated, 'That's the day I died,' and instantly was dead."

Before passing, this man not only made his own funeral arrangements, but he was able to give his father a very important message about a battle being fought, the welfare of his brother with regard to this battle, along with the health of the mother and children. He certainly did tie up loose ends before crossing over to the afterlife!

In the following account, another woman also knows when she will die. Her announcement of her upcoming death happens during a shopping trip.

On my last birthday, before she passed, my mom was alive and well. We had decided to spend my birthday shopping. During that shopping trip she told me she would pass on in six months. I said, "How do you know?" She then said to me, "You are not the only one who knows things. I know things too!" Six months later, to the day, she did pass to spirit.

The woman in this account intuitively knew her time for departure was near and had six months to prepare for this. Yes, if given the opportunity the dying will decide just when to pass on.

Let's take a look at one more of Barrett's accounts. In this interesting narrative, before joining her grandmother on the other side, a dying girl has a few things to take care of.

She knew she was passing away, and was telling our mother how to dispose of her little personal belongings among her close friends and playmates, when she suddenly raised her eyes as though gazing at the ceiling toward the farther side of the room, and after looking steadily and apparently listening for a short time, slightly bowed her head and said, "Yes, Grandma, I am coming, only wait just a little while, please." Our father asked her, "Hattie, do you see your grandma?" Seemingly surprised at the question she promptly answered, "Yes, Papa, can't you see her? She is right there waiting for me." At the same time she pointed toward the ceiling in the direction in which she had been gazing. Again addressing the vision she evidently had of her grandmother, she scowled a little impatiently and said, "Yes, Grandma, I'm coming, but wait a minute, please." She then turned once more to her mother and finished telling her what of her personal treasures to give to different ones of her acquaintances. At last giving her attention once more to her grandmother, who was apparently urging her to come at once, she bade each of us good-bye. Her voice was very feeble and faint, but the look in her eyes as she glanced briefly at each one of us was as lifelike and intelligent as it could be. She then fixed her eyes steadily on her vision but so faintly that we could just catch her words, said, "Yes, Grandma, I'm coming now."

According to the rest of the account found in Barrett's *Death-Bed Visions,* the little girl and her grandmother, who had passed several years previously, had been very close. Though her grandmother was insistent on her granddaughter joining her, little Hattie first had to make sure her belongings were carefully distributed to her playmates. Once her preparations were completed, she crossed the veil to join her awaiting grandmother. What a blessing it must have been for Hattie's parents to know their daughter was safe and sound with her favorite grandmother.

Instead of burying death and all that it entails behind the facade of false hope and flowery denial, we need to begin respecting the death experience. By embracing death as a spiritual adventure, we can begin to shed the prison of fear that has been built up over the last several generations. As a society, we really do need to return to this mode of preparedness for passage into the afterlife.

We will always grieve the passing of dear ones, but isn't it time for us to begin seeing death as a natural, normal, human experience? If we are willing to look death in the eye and investigate the nature of DBVs, ADCs and NDEs, we will be better prepared to assist our loved ones as they pass. Giving the dying a proper sendoff is one of the greatest of gifts. As Jonathan Swift said in his "Thoughts on Religion": "It is impossible that anything so natural, so necessary, and so universal as death should ever have been designed by Providence as an evil to mankind." Need I say more?

DBVs, Death Preparations and the Arts

The whole idea of preparing for death can be found throughout art, music, poetry and literature. My favorite piece of art was done by the eighteenth-century English artist and poet, William Blake. In this engraving, a woman is beautifully laid out on her bed. A second image of her is seen leaving the body. In the engraving is an open window, which looks out on to mountains. When I look at this picture, I am reminded of the passing of my very dear friend's father. This man knew he was dying and tried to make one final preparation for his trip.

My father-in-law suffered a massive heart attack. Being a physician, I was able to be in the operating room with him. As we tried to stabilize him, he began to gesture at me. He couldn't speak, but he was able to gesture. For the life of me, I couldn't understand what it was he wanted. Suddenly I figured it out. He wanted me to open a window. What was strange about this is that there was no way he could have known there was a window in the OR. It was never in his field of vision, but he was most adamant about this. I guess he knew he wasn't going to survive. He died minutes after this.

Did this dying man feel he needed to have an open window to exit through in order to reach an afterlife existence? As in the picture by Blake, the theme of opening a window for the dying is a common one. Read the next account from Barrett's *Death-Bed Visions.* This event took place at about 2 A.M. on July 28, 1881.

Just after dear Mrs. L.'s death between 2 and 3 A.M., I heard a most sweet and singular strain of singing outside the windows; it died away after passing the house. All in the room (except Mr. L., [the son]) heard it, and the medical attendant, who was still with us, went to the window, as I did, and looked out, but there was nobody. It was a bright and beautiful night. It was as if several voices were singing in perfect unison a most sweet melody which died away in the distance. Two persons had gone from the room to fetch something and were coming upstairs at the back of the house and heard the singing and stopped, saying, "What is that singing?" They could not naturally have heard any sound from outside the windows in the front of the house where they were at the back.

Here is another version of this same DBV, from the doctor who was present during the passing.

I remember the circumstance perfectly. I was sent for about midnight, and remained with Mrs. L. until her passing at about 2:30 A.M. Shortly after we heard a few bars of lovely music, not unlike that from an aeolian harp—and it filled the air for a few seconds. I went to the window thinking there must be someone outside, but could see no one though it was quite light and clear. Strangely enough, those outside the room heard the same sounds, as they were coming upstairs quite at the other side of the door (house).

This story is fascinating. First we have those at the deathbed who heard music coming from outside the window. When they go to see who is singing, nobody is there. Second, we find that others in the residence are not near the window, but on a staircase on the other side of the house, and they too hear the music. Finally, the son of the woman who has passed is at the deathbed, but unlike the others present in the room, he doesn't detect a note of music. It appears as though this departed soul received a musical escort as she began her journey!

Another cherished piece of art that relates to the dying experience was created by fifteenth-century Flemish artist Hieronymous Bosch, and is titled "Ascent into the Empyrearn." This work depicts souls moving through a tunnel toward a brilliant light. NDE researchers have long heard accounts of travel through tunnels toward incredible light. The notion of travel to a brilliant afterlife light has been with us for some time. Those experiencers who have returned from near death and been in the light find it difficult to express the joy, love and peace they encountered while in its presence. The following DBV account gives us a glimpse of travel to the light.

My father died in 1998. While at his funeral, my aunt (who my father lived with) and I were talking and she told me of the following conversation. This discussion had taken place before my father had died, and I found it to be most unusual.

My Aunt M. was visiting with my Aunt O. Both were quite religious, so they were sitting together at my father's house discussing something along that line. Meanwhile, my dad was sitting on the couch watching TV, but I guess he must have been half listening. During the conversation between my aunts, one said to the other, "You know they say when you die there is a tunnel and there is a light." The other aunt then said, "I have heard of that as well." Then my dad spoke up and said, "Yes, there is a light, I have seen that light and know that light." He said nothing more.

He never told me of this experience, but what is strange is that two weeks before his death, he started to do the rounds and visit everyone. As a matter of fact, on the Saturday before his death, I stayed at home because I knew, somehow, that he was coming to see me. We never made a date. I just somehow knew. He showed up on Sunday. He only stayed a few hours and then he had to go. My dad was strangely quiet, and I honestly believe he came to say

*good-bye to my husband and me. At the time, his visit
seemed weird. He seemed so sad. After hearing my aunts'
story, it all makes sense now.*

In this account, we have a man who somehow knows he
is going to pass. He begins preparing by visiting his loved
ones. He also knows the passage he will go through when
it is time for him to move on. In his vision (which sounds
like a near-death experience), he has seen the light.
Because he has seen "that light" he takes control of his
destiny and begins preparations for his departure.

Traveling

"I need to get packed for my trip" is an often-heard comment from the dying. It's as if they know they are going
somewhere and they need to prepare. In reviewing near-
death experiences, I have found a number of reports where
experiencers describe specific methods of travel to the
beyond. Dr. Moody, in his book *Life After Life,* provides a
colorful description of an otherworldly voyage. In this
account, a woman suffering from a post-partum hemor-
rhage had an NDE. After she is resuscitated, she has this to
say:

*On the distant shore, I could see all of my loved ones who
had died—my mother, my father, my sister and others. . . .*

They seemed to be beckoning me to come on over, and all the while I was saying, "No, no, I'm not ready to join you. I don't want to die. I'm not ready to go."

Moody reports further that this woman did not complete her ride to the other side. At the last minute, the ferry she had boarded turned around, and soon after that she found herself back in her body.

Some of the dying also seem to know where they are going to once they leave this plane of existence. In the quote at the beginning of chapter 6, van Gogh supposedly said, "Now I want to go home" as he lay dying. In reviewing DBVs, I have noticed that the notion of traveling "home" is a common theme.

My dear friend Troy shared another delightful story with me about his dying mother. She knew she was going home and she knew exactly what the term "home" meant. Here is the perfect example of how a family should treat the upcoming death of a loved one.

In about mid-January 1997 Mom was eating her lunch. At about that same time, her caregiver came into the room to check on her. Mom looked at her and then looked at me and said, "Yes, I know. I have to eat so I don't have to go back to the hospital." I then said, "Mom, you aren't going back to the hospital." She looked at me intently and then asked, "That means you agree with me that I am dying?" I answered, "Yes, you are." With this she responded, "Then why in the heck doesn't anyone else agree with me?"

On the afternoon of February 9, 1997, Mom looked at me and said, "When are you going to let me go home?" I explained that she was at home, where she had lived for fifty years. I then added that she was downstairs in the morning room, in a hospital bed, instead of upstairs in her bedroom. Initially I thought she believed she was back in Methodist Hospital. She looked me straight in the eye and said, "That's not what I mean," and then grinned.

I knew then, without a doubt, that she was ready to die. There was no question that Mom was comfortable with her pending death. This experience made me, my wife and my sister comfortable with her pending death.

On Sunday, February 23, after church services, I went to her home for our daily visit. She was sleeping, but was experiencing breathing difficulties. Both her caregiver and I agreed the time of her death was near. I kept talking to her because I believe people sleeping or in comas can still hear us. About mid-afternoon her breathing became more labored, shallow and slower. Finally she just quit.

Because of Troy's religious beliefs, along with his experience with his mother's passing, he truly believes she has gone home. "Home" in this case meant an afterlife plane of existence. Mother and son might be temporarily separated by the veil of death, but Troy feels quite comfortable knowing his mother is safe and sound.

Another NDE researcher explored the theme of going home in his collection of accounts. From Ring's *Heading Toward Omega* (1984) we read:

> *Peace. Homecoming. It's strange, because I never really verbalized that before. It was really like a homecoming. It was beautiful, it was magnificent. And it was so warm . . . another (kind of) warmth. An acceptance, a real acceptance.*

When my youngest son was a toddler, he often spoke of "going home" when he was upset. Like most youngsters, my son was no exception when it came to the terrible twos. During that time, when particularly agitated, he would often say, "I want to go home!" My reply would always be, "But honey, you are home!" With this he would sob and say, "No, I want to go back to my other home!" For a year or so this "other home" baffled all of us. Eventually I had one of those *Aha!* moments and recognized, "Yes, he probably did have another home before he came to live with us!" I have often wondered if the comments made by DBV and NDE experiencers about travel to "home" is in any way connected to the "other home" my son discussed in his early years. Could they be the same destination?

The dying's talk of travel often leaves survivors totally confused. We saw earlier how Troy's mother talked of going home. My friend Troy thought his mother was thinking she wasn't home because she was in a downstairs room of her home as opposed to her upstairs bedroom. Did she ever set him straight!

The following DBV account, which really gave me a chuckle, also involves a trip with a very determined traveler!

> My sister-in-law was her mother's primary caregiver at home during the last four months of her life. The last few days were nuts. Her mom wanted to know whether everything was ready for the trip. When my sister-in-law asked, "What trip?" her mom became very upset with her. My sister-in-law's mother thought her daughter should know without being told that she was leaving for Ireland.
>
> She humored her mom and asked who she was going with. Her mom then told her she was going with her husband and my sister-in-law's sister, both long deceased.
>
> The family is Irish and this woman had always considered Ireland as her "kind of heaven." My sister-in-law had to actually pack bags, and make excuses for why the passport wasn't updated. The one outfit her mom wanted to take was an outfit her husband had given to her years ago. "The weird thing is," said my sister-in-law, "I immediately knew which outfit it was she was talking about. I think it was about the only thing Dad ever bought for her."

Initially, the family didn't consider the many different aspects of this account to be related to a DBV. This Irish woman announced she was taking a trip and then appears to be confused because her daughter isn't aware of this.

The Irish woman then divulges to her daughter-in-law that she is taking this trip with her deceased husband and daughter. If this was just delusional thinking, why are the dying woman's travel companions not living family members?

Let's take a look at another DBV with a trip theme.

The day before my husband died, he became agitated and disoriented. He kept screaming at me to "pay the forty-nine dollars to get the car properly registered" and to "start packing up the car for a trip." He also told a dear friend of ours that he was going to be driving on another long cross-country trip. My husband always was the one who drove—everywhere. He and his late first wife had even gone to Alaska! He had driven there too! My husband often drove cross-country trips, nearly straight through—from San Francisco to New York, Tennessee to Seattle.

When death was imminent, I talked to him and sang to him. He had been unconscious for twelve hours—then, suddenly, he tightly squeezed my hand! Within an hour or so he passed away. I felt his spirit leave his body and hover above it for awhile. A few minutes later another dear friend came into the room and joined me. He and I both noted that we felt my husband's spirit still in the room.

Weeks after his death, I read a book titled Final Gifts. *In this book, the author mentioned many situations where the person who was dying spoke of different modes of travel such as plane tickets, train tickets, bus tickets and so on. Since my husband always drove everywhere, I really believe*

that he knew he was dying. He was going to drive our little
1989 blue Hyundai straight to the gates of heaven!

Because this woman found a copy of the book *Final Gifts*, she was able to discover that it is normal for the dying to discuss taking trips. In this case, the man who is passing is described as agitated, and it sounds as though he was desperate to make final preparations. To the unaware observer, it would most likely be determined that this particular man was just delusional. Thanks to the information provided in *Final Gifts* the wife of the dying man recognizes her husband wasn't delusional. This particular book has been a true gift for both the dying and those who love them.

The next DBV account comes from a businesswoman who was with her mother until she passed. Once again we are presented with a vision involving a trip. In this narrative, a dying woman wants to be totally prepared for her journey.

My mother passed two weeks ago this morning. She and
I were very close, and we had a couple of difficult nights
before she had her vision. Her vision took place during the
daytime. Two days prior to her passing, I was sitting in her
room alone with her. Suddenly, she began talking to some-
one, and that someone was not me. In an upbeat tone, she
said "Mother" twice, and then quite happily she answered,
"Okay." This was followed with, "I don't know."

Later on, my mother seemed annoyed and wanted to know from me, "When are we going to go?" I then replied, "Not just yet." Then she wanted to know what she was going to wear, and I told her what she had on was just fine. This seemed to satisfy her. A few minutes after this, she wanted to know about her pocketbook, and I told her I had it ready. I did note that her conversation with me after her vision was gentle, but uncharacteristically demanding. Shortly after this conversation, she lapsed into a deep sleep and then passed.

My mother's religious faith was very strong. She had told her minister that she was "ready to go" before I arrived to be with her. She always described herself as a fundamentalist Christian. I would not have been surprised if her deathbed vision had been that of an angel. It did surprise me that her mother, who was not only a wonderful person, but very close to my mother, had appeared! What a gift to have witnessed this!

I feel as though I have seen a door open for just a few seconds and I will never be the same. I believe our society needs to rethink how we deal with the process of passing. It shouldn't happen in hospitals unless circumstances make it absolutely necessary.

Today, I am at peace—hurting, but at peace—and I know beyond a shadow of a doubt that mother is also at peace.

This woman was able to glimpse where her mother was going after she died. Having her deceased grandmother visit her mother during the vision brought a sense of peace to both her and her mother. Also, we once again see how preparation for the upcoming trip was essential for another departing soul. The experience provided a spiritual awakening for the surviving daughter. Her mother's DBV has opened her up to a strong belief in an afterlife.

* * *

Modern science tells us there is no concrete proof of life after death. Many thinkers see a belief in the afterlife as superstitious behavior based on people's inability to accept nonexistence. Some researchers have made a career "proving" life after death does not exist. My question to these particular individuals is this: If life after death truly does not exist, why do the dying have such incredible visions? Why do many of these visions involve communications from those who already made the afterlife journey? How come many of the survivors feel so incredibly touched by such experiences? And finally, if death does not involve a journey, why is it that so many of the dying are aware they are soon going to be traveling?

William Blake produced a wonderful piece of art that depicts souls climbing up and down a golden stairway. Some of the golden-colored beings have wings and carry books, others appear to be bearing drink or food. Where on "Earth" did such a lovely image come from?

Chapter 9

Split Between Two Worlds

"Don't be afraid."

Parting words of Charles XII of Sweden

Some researchers suggest that a heightened sense of awareness emerges as the dying process plays itself out. As death approaches, is it possible that the world of the unknown is opened up to many of the dying and their family members? Emily Dickinson said with her last breath, "I must go. The fog is rising." As the fog of this final passage began to rise, just what did Dickinson see?

HEIGHTENED AWARENESS

The belief that extrasensory experiences become more prevalent as death approaches has been with humankind for as long as can be remembered. Ancient civilizations often turned to the dying for messages from the beyond. Anthropologist Ronald Rose studied Australian aborigines and discovered the mysterious psychic power that death has on both the living and the dying, as shown below.

> *Some strange beliefs have developed around the fact of dying. One, for example, is that the dying man becomes suddenly invested with a clairvoyant ability of the most extraordinary kind. . . . Even the sophisticated native believes that the one occasion during his life on which he can know the answer to any question is three days after his mother's death. He must stand at the foot of the grave and ask his question.*

This quote about the death beliefs of the Australian aborigines, taken from Rose's *Living Magic* (1957), gives us something to think about. I must agree with Rose. My most psychic moments have taken place just before, during or just after the passing of a close family member or friend. I don't think I'm alone in this experience.

We must begin asking ourselves whether or not the dying are actually more aware than we realize. If they are getting a glimpse of heaven, shouldn't we be listening more closely to what they have to say? Take a look at the following recent DBV account. If this story doesn't send chills down your spine, at least it will give you an opportunity to wonder.

My grandfather was on his deathbed. A couple of minutes
before he passed he said to my brother, "I see your father in
a uniform standing beside me." Then he looked up, smiled
and passed away. My father was still alive at that time.

Two years later my father was taken suddenly and guess
what he was wearing when he died? His uniform!

What clairvoyant abilities did the grandfather have as he
passed? Are the aborigines right? If so, doesn't our society
as a whole—including medical people, the clergy and
mental health professionals—need to be more mindful of
the final words of the dying? Let me present another interesting DBV. Take particular note of the prediction of the
woman who passed. This narrative comes from a nurse
who admits at the time of her patient's passing that she
was not able to take what was shared at face value.

A little lady was on a heart monitor after suffering a heart
attack. I worked the night shift that night and that evening,
and every time I made my rounds, I would find her talking
to the curtain in her room. I would ask her who she was
talking to and she would say, "You can't see her. She is so
beautiful, all in white. She is an angel, come to take me
home tonight."

I tried to explain her vision away by moving the curtain
back and showing her it was only the curtain, that there was
no one there. Today, I'm sorry I didn't believe her.

She continued to talk through the night. At about 5 A.M.

I went into her room to check her vital signs. She smiled at me and said, "I must be going now. Everything I needed to do here has been taken care of. For me it is time to go with my angel." She then took my hand and said, "You will do so much for others, even when you are in pain." With that, she smiled and closed her eyes. The alarms sounded and her heart stopped. . . . I will never forget that night.

She was right about my helping others even in my own pain. In May 1998 I lost my fifteen-year-old daughter in an auto accident. Today, my daughter sends me signs that she too still lives on.

To find comfort in the knowledge of a life after death, this nurse turns to the prediction given to her by her dying patient and her experiences with her own dying daughter. Yes, in spite of her own pain, today this woman helps others who have lost loved ones.

We have seen how the gift of the DBV visits the dying, but what about those who are at the bedside? Are the treasures of such visitations also bestowed on the living? Do the caregivers, family and friends of the one transitioning see "things" before a loved one passes? If so, do we as a society also need to be opening ourselves up more to these particular individuals? Couldn't we learn a great deal from them too? Will there ever come a time when the DBVs of both the departing and their survivors are commonly and candidly discussed? I sure hope so.

The Sixth Sense

During the summer of 1999, a movie hit the screens and became a Hollywood blockbuster. When I initially saw this film advertised in the local newspaper, I immediately thought to myself, *Here we go again! Guess Tinseltown has found a new well to dig! Seeing dead people! Why does the movie business have to involve itself in an area of the human experience I honor and take very seriously?* At the time, I was not pleased.

The movie was titled *The Sixth Sense,* and it told the tale of young boy who saw the spirits of those who had died. With no more information, I had already decided I wasn't going to watch this movie and made a point of telling my husband. "Blood, guts and gore? The dead terrorizing the living? *Pass!*" The thought of seeing one more typical Hollywood horror flick just wasn't on my dance card. Am I stubborn? Yes, but in due time, I was to learn my initial notion regarding this particular film was way off-base.

That same summer, hurricane Brett decided to bear down on the Texas Gulf Coast. At first glance, the whirling mass of strong wind, tornadoes and torrential rain appeared to be headed straight for our little island! Taking these storms quite seriously, my family and I had jumped into action in order to prepare for a possible date with Brett. Luckily, the storm made a sudden left-hand turn in south Texas and came ashore into no-man's land.

The adrenaline rush of fear the hurricane had created left Michael and I emotionally wrung out. For a cure to our Brett-lessness, we decided to take in a film. I had wanted to see a comedy, but somehow we ended up viewing *The Sixth Sense*. As I stuffed my face with popcorn, I noticed how captivated the audience was with this film. Aside from a few glitzy special effects, the movie was quite interesting. I was pleasantly surprised.

What affected me more than the film itself was the audience's attentiveness. The desire to understand life after death was engraved on the faces of most people in the movie theater. These moviegoers also appeared to have a great sense of compassion for the main character. The little boy in the film felt tortured by the deceased on the other side. He didn't understand why he was able to see them, and he was extremely frightened. Eventually, he discovers these souls don't really want to hurt him. They only want to talk with him.

The film put forth two very important points, the first being that the supposedly unseen world *can* be seen. Countless reports exist of everyday individuals seeing the deceased and even communicating with them. The first eight chapters of this book present only a very small sample of documented cases. The *Journal of the American Society for Psychical Research* has been investigating such visions since 1885. This particular organization has in its archives many, many documented cases of this nature.

The second point the film made is that those who can see the spirits of the deceased are often misunderstood. Years ago I worked with a woman who could see those living in the afterlife. As a matter of fact, these gabby folks overwhelmed her. For years she had used alcohol to block them out. Once sober, she didn't know how to hold them back! After hearing her incredible pain, I decided to teach her how to meditate. With meditation she could set limits, put up boundaries and say "Not now!" when she needed to.

She shared her therapy sessions with a friend of hers who, unfortunately, was extremely single-minded when it came to religion. Basically, her friend's philosophy went something like this: "It's my way or the highway to hell!" This particular woman was not pleased to learn I was teaching meditation to her friend. Instead of supporting my already confused client, she reacted with disdain and told her she was possessed by the devil!

At this time, I started hearing some bizarre rumors about myself in the community. The woman who was upset with my suggestion of meditation was telling people I was into black magic! I even started to hear from other clients that I was being accused of practicing black witchcraft in my office. It became painfully obvious to me that my client's predicament had been misunderstood, while my own attempts to remedy the situation were taken totally out of context. Sadly, this tale is not that uncommon. I strongly suspect that if my client had visited a traditional, medically oriented mental-health-care provider, she would have received a schizophrenia diagnosis and been loaded up on antipsychotic medications.

After a number of puzzling and often pain-racked years, this gifted woman was eventually able to embrace and accept her ability to see those on the other side. Today, she is open about it and has been able to serve others. *The Sixth Sense* provided the general public a quick peek at what life is like for such individuals. More awareness will hopefully in time bring a bit more acceptance.

BEDSIDE VISIONS

Up to this point, we have been discussing the visions of the dying. After reading through all of the accounts presented in this book, I suspect that even the most skeptical of skeptics would have to admit that the dying are seeing *something!* At this point, I would like to broaden your horizons even more. Continue your journey as we review the incredible experiences the living have had as they have watched their loved ones pass.

As mentioned earlier, Michael and my cousin Yvonne

both observed the misty spirits of their parents leave the body as their loved ones moved on to the afterlife. Michael saw a pastel mist rise from his father's body, while Yvonne witnessed a gray mist leave her dying mother as she passed. The following DBV account, experienced by a nurse, describes another such vision.

I was working with a woman who was dying of a terminal illness. One day I saw something really strange. I know you will think I'm nuts, but I saw a white cloud sort of hanging over the woman's bed. I could see it, but if I went to feel it, there was nothing to feel! I'm wondering if it was an angel. I really don't know. It was the strangest thing!

From Barrett's *Death-Bed Visions*, we read about a comparable encounter. The wording may be a bit different, but the content of the vision is exactly the same as the one described above.

In a letter that has recently been sent to me of a late well-known dignitary of the church (a dean) in New South Wales, he describes the death of his son a few years ago.

He says that at about 3:30 P.M. he and his wife were standing one on each side of the bed and bending over their dying son, when just as his breathing ceased they both saw, "something rise as it were from his face like a delicate veil or mist, and slowly pass away." He adds, "We were deeply impressed and remarked, 'How wonderful!' Surely that must be the departure of his spirit. We were not at all distracted so as to be mistaken in what we saw."

Here is another brief narration of what a woman recently witnessed at the moment of a loved one's death.

I saw his soul depart and this gave me peace of mind. He was pain-free and happily with his family.

Are these survivors really seeing "something" leave the body at the moment of death? In his book, *A Practical Guide to Death and Dying* (1988), John White wrote about such occurrences from a scientific perspective.

Another kind of (scientific) deathbed observation involves careful weighing of dying persons. The first study was made in 1907 by Harvard psychologist, Dr. William McDougall. He found an inexplicable sudden weight loss of about an ounce at the moment of expiration. Recently, a doctor in England and another in West Germany made the same observation. The weight loss, they said, could not be explained anatomically or physiologically. Apparently something leaves the body quite suddenly at the moment of death—something that weighs more than the air normally in the lungs.

That something may have been photographed by a Frenchman named Baraduc at the beginning of (the twentieth century). He made several photographs of his dying son, and six months later when his wife passed on, he did the same for her. In both instances, Baraduc's photographs show a cloudlike substance concentrated a little way above the dying body. These photos have never been explained away by parapsychologists or skeptics.

BEDSIDE VISITATIONS

These cloudlike substances aren't the only unusual occurrences to take place at the deathbed. Along with these particular accounts, many caretakers at the bedside have provided numerous descriptions of visions of angels and deceased relatives. It would appear as though those leaving us for the afterlife are not the only ones who receive otherworldly visitations.

My fifteen-year-old son died this past August (1998). He had a terminal illness. . . . We had encountered many life-and-death situations prior to this event. When this (event) happened, something told me this time was different and I knew he was going to die.

He was hospitalized with pneumonia. On Thursday he was put on a ventilator. When this happened, I told my son it was now his choice. He could go be with God, Jesus and the angels if he wanted to. I let him know he didn't have to do this anymore if he didn't want to.

On Saturday, he coded (heart stopped) but then he came back. During this time, my husband and I were sitting by his side. It was about 1:00 P.M. and I kept sensing something behind me. I kept turning around and looking. The sensation grew stronger each time I turned around. The third or fourth time I turned around, I saw my father, who had passed away thirteen years ago, standing in the doorway of my son's room.

He was as big as life. I saw such detail. I even remember seeing his shoelaces. He appeared to be brown and gold in color and there was a glow around his body. I didn't say anything to him. For a moment, I just stared at him. Then I turned to look at my son. As soon as I laid my eyes on my son, his heart failed. The doctors quickly rushed us out of the room and proceeded to work on his body for fifteen minutes. While this was happening, I was crying and saying, "It's okay, he can go."

I thank God for this experience. My son was very close to his Papa, who often appeared to him throughout his young life. I was close to my father and I often wondered why I never saw him. Then I did.

I knew as they worked on my son's body that he had already gone to heaven. This is only one of many spiritual experiences that occurred with our walk with death. My son had many visions and dreams prior to his death. He kept a journal and he had a near-death experience fifteen months prior to his actual death. He left his body and flew down the tunnel toward the bright light.

This mother had a visitation from her deceased father. Seeing him brought her a "knowing" that her son's departure was near. The encounter also provided her with great comfort.

The following narrative provides us with another curious story of a caretaker having visions at the bedside. The next example comes to us from Barrett's 1926 collection. In this account the caretaker of Laura, a very ill girl, has a fantastic vision. A powerful experience, the vision brings a new understanding of death to the woman at her side. This particular case was originally documented by Joy Snell in her book *The Ministry of Angels* (1918).

It was about six months after I began work in the hospital that it was revealed to me that the dying often really do see those who have come from the realms of spirit life to welcome them on their entrance into another state of existence.

The first time I received this ocular (visual) proof was at the death of Laura Stirman, a sweet girl of seventeen, who was a personal friend of mine. She was a victim of consumption. She suffered no pain, but the weariness that comes from extreme weakness and debility was heavy upon her and she yearned for rest.

A short time before she expired I became aware that two spirit forms were standing by the bedside, one on either side of it. I did not see them enter the room; they were standing by the bedside when they first became visible to me, but I could see them as distinctly as I could any of the human occupants of the room. I recognized their faces as those of two girls who had been the closest friends of the girl who was dying. They had passed away a year before and were then about her own age.

Just before they appeared the dying girl exclaimed, "It has grown suddenly dark; I cannot see anything!" But she recognized them immediately. A smile, beautiful to see, lit up her face. She stretched forth her hands and in joyous tones exclaimed, "Oh, you have come to take me away! I am glad, for I am very tired."

As she stretched forth her hands the two angels extended each a hand, one grasping the dying girl's right hand, the other her left hand. Their faces were illuminated by a smile more radiantly beautiful even than that of the girl who was so soon to find the rest for which she longed. She did not speak again, but for nearly a minute her hands remained outstretched, grasped by the hands of the angels, and she continued to gaze at them with the glad light in her eyes and the smile on her face.

Her father, mother, and brother, who had been summoned that they might be present when the end came, began weeping bitterly, for they knew that she was leaving them. From my heart there went up a prayer that they (the grieving family) might see what I saw, but they could not.

The angels seemed to relax their grasp of the girl's hands, and which then fell back on the bed. A sigh came from her lips, such as one might give who resigns himself gladly to a much-needed sleep, and in another moment she was what the world calls dead. But that sweet smile with which she had first recognized the angels was still stamped on her features.

The two angels remained by the bedside during the brief space that elapsed before the spirit form took shape above the body in which physical life had ceased. Then they rose and stood for a few moments on each side of her, who was now like unto themselves: and three angels went from the room where a short time before there had been only two.

Not only did the caretaker see the deceased friends of this young woman, but she saw the spirit of the girl above her body moments after her death.

Let's now compare this account with another encounter. Like Barrett's description from Joy Snell, the following vision is also witnessed by a caretaker sitting at the side of the dying. In this particular case, a husband witnesses his wife's departure from this world. As you will see, this woman definitely didn't leave the earth plane by herself. Instead, she was given a grand escort to the other side by a very loving group of otherworldly beings.

I was at my wife's side when she passed over, and I saw, felt and experienced her transition.

She was escorted into spirit realm by a very large number of Light Beings, far more than I could count. Her transition was very easy and very beautiful. She was quite ready and prepared. She went directly to the heart of God.

I have had many, many experiences and communications with my late wife since she passed on, but that was the only experience I had at the time of her passing. I can assure you that my brief words do not even begin to express the beauty and wonder of what I saw and felt at her passing.

With this DBV, Bob states that he "saw, felt and experienced" his wife's transition to the other side. I have listened to others speak of "feeling" their loved one leaving. One woman told me she experienced her husband's entire death process. She stated that in an after-death communication (ADC) with him, he had wanted her to know what he had gone through when he died. His hope was that the experience would give her peace of mind.

With regard to such an adventure, here is another DBV encounter to consider. Instead of having a visual experience, this narrative presents the sensation a woman felt as she held her dying daughter's hand.

> *I don't know if this is something worth noting or if it has nothing to do with anything, but here goes. I was holding my M—'s hand close to the time of her passing and I felt a continuous vibration, like a buzzing sensation.*

Like Bob, the above woman felt a physical sensation at the moment of her daughter's death. Can we feel our loved ones leaving the body? In some cases I think, "Yes!"

Bob also had a wonderful vision. As his beloved wife left him, he saw her being cared for by a multitude of loving beings from the afterlife. Watching his wife be assisted in this way was not only comforting, but set him on a firm path as a health giver. Today, Bob is very dedicated to being of service to others who have lost a loved one. His kind, spiritual guidance has provided a great deal of healing direction for many.

For family and friends who have had DBVs of their own, seeing is believing. In some cases, for a grieving survivor, just hearing about what another has seen can be very affirming. Let's look at another one of Joy Snell's cases, as presented in Barrett's book. This account is authored by the same woman who narrated the DBV about the two angels. Because death was common in her line of work, this woman would naturally have had more exposure to such experiences. Notice how her reported vision affects the other person sitting at this particular deathbed.

After I left the hospital and had taken up private nursing I was engaged to nurse an old lady (Mrs. Barton, age sixty), who was suffering from a painful internal disease. She was a widow and her only daughter lived with her. . . . The time came when the end was very near. The mother had been for some time unconscious, and the daughter was kneeling by the bedside, weeping, her face buried in her hands. Suddenly two angels became visible to me, standing on either side of the bed. The face of one was that of a man who, when he departed from this life, was apparently about sixty years of age. The face of the other angel was that of a woman, apparently some ten to fifteen years younger.

The dying woman opened her eyes, and into them there came that look of glad recognition. She stretched forth her two hands. One angel grasped one hand and the other angel the other hand, while their radiant faces were aglow with the joy of welcoming [one] to the better world. [H]er . . . earthly pilgrimage was finished.

"Oh, Willie," she exclaimed, "you have come to take me home at last, and I am glad, for my sufferings have been hard to bear. . . ." Then she added, "And you too, Martha!" All her sufferings were over.

The daughter had raised her head at the sound of her mother's voice, and her tear-dimmed eyes seemed to reflect something of the glad surprise depicted on her mother's face.

"I can doubt no more after this," she said to me when her mother had breathed her last breath. "I know that Mother saw Father and her sister, Aunt Martha. I know that they came to take her to her rest in heaven."

Eagerly she listened to me when I told her a little later how I had seen two angels depart with her angel mother. "I believe it! I believe it!" she cried, "but oh, how I wish that I could have seen it too!"

In the vision received by this woman, she sees two angels. The dying widow calls out to these two by name. The daughter later identifies the "angels" in the DBV as her father and her mother's sister. The widow passes gently and the daughter at her side is greatly consoled. Did the nurse caretaker really see these two deceased relatives? Take a look at another DBV. Note what this woman witnessed and the similarities to Snell's narrative.

Like Bob, the caretakers sitting at these deathbeds see angels. Can we so readily dismiss three separate visions?

My beloved dad died on April 23, 1999. What gives me comfort is what happened during the last four days of his life. My sister and I flew to Florida to be with him because he was in a coma and his condition was grave. The first day and all four subsequent days, I sensed an angel standing at the head of his bed waiting to take him home. I cannot tell you how comforting this was as my dad was really suffering.

A few hours before his death I heard my grandmother calling his name over and over again. I sensed she was standing at the foot of his bed touching his feet, calling him and telling him it was okay and it was time to go.

The next DBV case creates many questions for the "it was just a dream" or the "overactive imagination" theory. The woman in this account had several otherworldly visitations before her own mother's death.

I personally feel that the dying have certain experiences before death and that family members can also have such experiences. Three months prior to my mom's death, I was awakened from a sleep hearing a female voice calling my name. I went to my mom's bedroom to see if it was her and it wasn't.

Six weeks later we were on vacation in a cabin in West Virginia and the same thing happened again. I heard a voice calling. My mom was at home when this happened.

The third time it happened, my mom was in the intensive care unit.

Who was calling this woman? Was she being forewarned from the beyond that her mother was going to pass?

The next DBV account was given to me by my good friend Valerie. When her father was passing, he sent an urgent message for her to go to him. Her message did not come to her by way of a letter, telegram, e-mail or phone call. Her father needed her and there wasn't time for modern technology. Up until this point, Valerie had not been aware that her father was preparing to die.

My family and I were in a Kentucky restaurant on the Ohio River at exactly 5 P.M. A man who looked almost exactly like my father was seated directly across from me. I couldn't avoid looking directly at him and as I did, something told me to look directly at this stranger. As I did my vision of him became fuzzy and suddenly I was seeing my father.

Now my thoughts were on my dad and as I focused on him I felt my dad in my heart area. It felt tingling and it was if my dad was pulling on me, trying to pull me out of my body. I knew there had to be an explanation for this feeling, but I couldn't put my finger on it.

Tears started pouring down my face. One of my sons said, "Mom, what's the matter?" I had finally figured out that there was an explanation for this pulling sensation from my father and answered, "I think I'm having a mystical experience and I have to go to Florida to be with Granddad."

My sons said something to the effect of, "No, you are not! This is only happening because that man sitting over there looks a little bit like Granddad!" Then I said, "That man was sitting there for a reason. He is there to trigger me. I know this for a fact."

When we arrived home, I immediately called the hospital to inquire about my dad's health. The nurses explained to me that dad had begun to have trouble breathing at precisely 5:00 P.M., and had been placed in a medically induced coma to keep him from fighting the respirator he had been put on.

Upon hearing this, I know my father, at that moment in time, had refused to die. He had come to get me so that Marty (my husband) and I could go to Florida to take care of my mother and the details when he did die. He refused to die until we got there.

Because of various complications, Marty and I couldn't get to my parent's house until 1 A.M. Sunday morning. Just as Marty came into the house (I had arrived just a bit earlier by airplane), and was beginning to relax after his drive, the hospital called to say that dad was in crisis; his kidneys had failed. I knew instinctively this was my call for action. So, Marty and I led Mother to the car for the drive to the hospital.

Dad's heart stopped at 4 A.M. on Sunday morning. I am certain his spirit left his body on the previous Tuesday, at 5 P.M., and made its way to the restaurant in Kentucky where it then entered my chest area. He must have bargained with the Powers That Be so that Marty and I could be with Mom when he passed. My mom was in total denial of the severity of the situation and would have been incapable of making the necessary decisions after Dad's death. He knew we needed to be there to support her.

When my dad died, he was at peace with Marty, me, Mom,

the doctors, the nurses and the chaplain, surrounding him.
My dad had called and I came.

I know this experience had a profound effect on both Marty and Valerie. Today the two of them are very open to such experiences. Valerie is also extremely involved with IANDS, the International Association for Near-Death Studies. Valerie's dad needed her to be by his side as he passed. Though his body was laying in a hospital bed in Florida, he paid her a special visit in Kentucky.

VISITS FROM THE DYING

Angels and surrogate figures aren't the only otherworldly beings making appearances at deathbeds. There are numerous reports of the dying visiting the living before making a final departure. Many of these visitations come in full Technicolor! A relative of mine shared the following story:

My mother was dying in west Texas. At that time, one of my sisters was living in Erie, Pennsylvania. She was not aware that my mother was passing, but the night she died, my sister had an unusual experience.

My sister said she was abruptly awakened from a very deep sleep. When she woke up, she said her body felt frozen and she couldn't open her eyes. Suddenly she felt a presence in the room and knew it was Mother. She felt her standing at the foot of the bed.

A short time later, we called her to tell her Mother passed. She then asked us what time it was when Mother died. When we told her, she said she had felt our mother's presence in the bedroom at that exact moment.

This aunt knew her mother was in west Texas, but at the moment of passing felt her mother's spirit in her bedroom in Pennsylvania.

Compare this DBV account with one presented in Tom Harpur's book, *Life After Death* (1991). Do you notice any similarities?

D. W. lived in Owen Sound, Ontario, and his mother was quite ill in a hospital in London, over 150 kilometers away. He was driving down to visit her and stopped overnight at his aunt's home in Goderich. In the middle of the night he was awakened to see his mother as a younger woman standing at the foot of the bed. She told him she had come to say good-bye. In the morning when he got up, his aunt informed him that his mother had died during the night. He knew that "it hadn't been a dream; it had really been her."

Was this "good-bye" experience really a visit from a mother who was about to walk through the door to the afterlife? Did she feel a need to let her son know she was passing before she left?

Skeptics may say that such cases are only the by-product of dream material, overactive imaginations or the result of the emotional exhaustion of having a family member who is dying. Somehow this explanation just seems too simplistic. Cases such as these are common, and as always the visitations seem to have a specific purpose. I believe many of the dying visit their loved ones as they pass because they feel they need to.

Another DBV account of this nature comes from *Life After Death*. See if you can determine why this grandmother felt it was necessary to pay her grandson a visit before she left this world.

B. Y., who says he was raised in the United Church of Canada but always felt very skeptical about such beliefs as those concerning life after death, had been very close to his grandmother as a boy. He was in his early twenties and recently married when he learned that she was quite ill in a hospital in a northern town miles away. One morning, he awoke very early and saw his grandmother standing at the entrance to his bedroom. "She was wearing the mauve suit that I always recognized as one of her favorites. Her face was very taut and sunken and would have looked terrible had it not been for the fact that she looked joyful at the same time. She just stood there silently. I closed my eyes before taking another look. She was gone but the phone began to ring. It woke my wife—it was on her side of the bed—and as she reached for it, I told her, 'Grandma is dead.' She picked the phone up and my aunt told her what I already knew."

The grandson in the above account was skeptical of a belief in an afterlife. It appears as though his grandmother took care of that! It would be difficult to say that his vision of his grandmother was a product of wishful thinking. Unfortunately some people would go to great lengths to debate this point. I tend to believe this grandmother wanted her beloved grandson to know she was joyously happy on the other side.

I believe love crosses all boundaries. It doesn't end with our last breath. Doesn't it make sense that the dying would want to comfort us in our grief, especially if we have had a loving relationship with them in life?

In another DBV story, a visitation is made upon a man while he is driving in his car, awake and fully alert.

I was driving down the road to get money from the bank machine so that I could hop on a plane first thing in the morning. It was dark outside and my son was laying in a hospital in California with a bullet in his head. The doctor gave him no chance to live.

Suddenly, the glove box flew open. John is dead, *I said in my heart.* This is a sign. *As I closed the glove box, I heard a voice say, "I didn't mean to hurt anyone." I looked to my right and there was John's face, shining in the darkness.*

"I know you didn't, John, I know you didn't," I replied.

His face moved closer, until it was about a foot from my head. "I am so sorry," he said.

"I know you are, John. I know you are," I replied.

His face started to move again. Suddenly I felt his arm around my back, as he hugged me tightly and told me how much he loved me.

"I love you too," I replied. "I love you very much. . . ."

While this man was traveling in his car and talking to his son, at home his wife received a phone call from the hospital, telling her their son had just died. This indeed was one last hug from a son who knew it was his time to move on. Not only did he inform his father that he was leaving him, but he came to make an apology.

Can the dying come to survivors with last-minute messages? Closely examine the DBV Tom Harpur documented in *Life After Death*.

S. B. describes a time she was on a bus with some friends in London, England: "A woman opened a car door on the wrong side and a man on a bicycle swerved violently to avoid a collision. So did the bus driver. The bus hit the cyclist and dragged him some distance before coming to a stop on the sidewalk. We were pretty shaken and everybody was staring, not doing anything. I got off the bus and tried to help the young man. Someone ran to call an ambulance and I covered him with my coat. He was fully conscious so I sat on the curb . . . and tried to console him. Later that night, I was in bed reading at about 2 A.M. when this man appeared. I was

*scared at first but all he did was to mouth "Thank you."
There was no sound. I was still shaken the next day when the
papers reported the accident and said he had died at 2 A.M.*

Proper manners till the very end! In this situation, the
woman didn't know the man who had the accident.
Obviously he felt he could not move on until he properly
thanked her for her kindness.

Spirit Visitations

We have seen how the dying will visit the living. As the
moment of death draws near, do otherworldly beings also
visit friends and family members? Read through the next
account taken from *Life After Death.*

*A. M. writes that fifteen years ago she was very ill at home.
One day she awoke to find a tall, well-dressed man standing
just outside her bedroom door. When she looked at him, he
asked, "Are you ready?" "I quickly said, 'No,'" she relates. For
many years, she supposed she had dreamed this odd incident. Seven years ago, her husband was diagnosed as having
terminal cancer. Near the end, she brought him home from
hospital as he had expressed a deep wish to die at home.*

*"As our two sons helped the ambulance men to carry my
husband to the bedroom, he pointed to the same spot where
I had seen the stranger (fifteen years ago) and asked me,
'Who is he?' When I asked him later who was who, he*

described the same well-dressed man I had seen years before. I have never told anyone about this, but felt I had to write. No, I do not know who this man was, and as we bought the house new thirty years ago no one else had lived here. I still wonder who this stranger was."

In this narrative we have a mysterious being visiting both the living and the dying. Was the stranger in this woman's home there to help her husband cross over to the afterlife? Barrett's research on DBVs related that when dying children received visitations from angels, the angels didn't have wings. Was this well-dressed wingless creature an angel from beyond? Compare the above account with the following DBV narrative.

Approximately three days before my husband died, my daughter had a friend visit the house. This friend said she saw a man walk across our yard and then knock on our front door. When she went to open the door, no one was there. The reason I brought this up is that many years ago my husband told me a story about a man who saw the angel of death walk from his yard to his neighbor's yard and then he just disappeared. His son and his neighbor's son died shortly afterwards. I am wondering if the person my daughter's friend saw and heard knocking on the door was in fact an angel.

Obviously the living also have DBVs. In reviewing the above accounts, it is difficult to deny that some people are quite susceptible to such visitations. What lessons can we learn from these otherworldly visitations? These visions tell the true tale of death. With death there really is nothing to fear. Generations before us knew this intuitively. Why is our scientifically minded generation so quick to debate and discount what we the experiencers have felt, seen and heard with our own senses?

The next DBV was experienced by the grandchildren of a dying grandmother. Hopefully, like the grandchildren in this account, future generations will feel comfortable openly embracing messages from the world beyond.

> *The doctors from the ICU called to tell me that Mom had slipped back into a coma and that her death was near. This was at about 5:30 A.M. My husband had just left for work and there was no one at home but my daughter, my son and myself.*
>
> *I had just hung up the telephone and we were all in the dining room. Suddenly, our front door opened and closed. My son went to see who it was and there was no one there. I told my children that their grandmother had come home. My mother grew up in the house we lived in and had continued living there until she was seventy-five. It has been my home for forty-nine years, all of my life.*
>
> *I will always believe that my mom came home that morning.*

This woman's children also witnessed the opening and closing of the door. The family is convinced Grandma paid them an early-morning visit, just before she made her way to the other side. Such messages from those who have passed or are passing are for the most part very consoling to survivors. These encounters tend to provide a great deal of peace for all those concerned.

I have often wondered if those in the afterlife are frustrated with certain members of our stubborn generation. It would be very upsetting to me if my attempts to contact and comfort those I cared for were dismissed. Why should it be any different for loved ones on the other side? In this final account, we watch as a widow finally recognizes that her late husband has been trying to get her attention for some time.

Ever since my dear husband passed, I have had the strangest experiences. On either side of my bed, I have a nightstand. Periodically, this really bizarre rattling noise comes from one of them. Believe me, both my son and I have checked this nightstand out from top to bottom. Nothing can explain the funny sounds that come from it. What is especially unusual about this is that the rattling noise only comes just before someone I know passes.

My son and I have often felt my husband's presence in the house. During these times, the dog senses something too, because he starts barking like mad. I have often wondered if the rattling is my husband's way of warning me of an upcoming death.

When I last talked to this woman, her nightstand had been rattling again. Today she pays very close attention to this sign from her husband. We will see if anyone she knows and loves crosses over in the near future.

Glimpses of Heaven

In researching deathbed visions, Osis and Haraldsson not only encountered reports of otherworldly angels, religious figures and deceased relatives. They also came across a number of accounts of other "heavenly" landscapes. In researching visions, I too have noted descriptions of "indescribable," "beautiful," "serene," "brilliant" and "peaceful" vistas. Even during ancient times, beautiful descriptions of the other side have been related back to the living by the dying. Johannes Bronsted's book *The Vikings* offers one description of what life after death looks like.

In 922 A.D., an Arab ambassador was living in a Viking community where a Viking chief had been buried. In this account, as translated by Ambassador Ibn Fadlan's interpreter, the dead chief's slave woman was about to die so that she could be with her master. During this time the slave woman was elevated up on to a special frame three times. As her death approached, here is what the interpreter reported to the ambassador. This DBV describes a world the slave woman would be welcomed into at the moment of death.

The first time they lifted her she said, "Look! I see my father and mother." The second time she said, "Look! I see all my dead relatives sitting around." The third time she said, "Look! I see my master sitting in paradise, and paradise is beautiful and green and together with him are men and young boys. He calls on me. Let me join them!"

Nurses and doctors at the deathbed of a patient often encounter descriptions of the beyond. After having read the otherworldly description above, see if you detect any similarities between it and the following DBV accounts from Osis and Haraldsson's *At the Hour of Death.*

She saw open gates and felt she was going to a place with flowers, lights, colors, and a lot of beauty. She was annoyed with me for disturbing her and accused me of not permitting her to get in this place. She was thrilled with (the vision) and angry at me.

* * *

An unusual patient, very alert and intellectual, keen sense of humor . . . a down-to-earth person. That morning . . . she told me that . . . she (had seen) beautiful, endless gardens (with) all kinds of flowers. She said that she had never seen anything like it, it was gorgeous. She did not want to return (from this place).

* * *

The patient said, "It looked like a great sunset, very large and beautiful." The clouds suddenly appeared to be gates. She felt that somebody was calling her to them, that she had to go through (them).

* * *

When he had visions the pain would disappear and all you could see was a smile on his face. He would say, "It was so beautiful, you just can't tell anyone. It was a breath-taking scene, more so than anything in real life." That was all he could say.

* * *

The patient found herself up in the sky. It looked like clouds. She was walking on clouds. She saw many castles there. They were in bright light, very beautiful. She was so impressed with their beauty.

In all five of these accounts, the health-care profession-als at the deathbed heard the patient use either the word "beauty" or "beautiful" to describe what they were seeing. When Osis and Haraldsson compared the otherworldly visions of Americans with those from individuals born in India, they discovered the two cultures had similar fea-tures. Both groups reported seeing gates, trees, castles, buildings, gardens, temples, streams and flowers.

As the dying talk about their visions of these landscapes,

the descriptions appear to be intensified with color, illuminated with light and seen as beyond perfection. These lovely visions of life after death are incredibly inviting. Combine this with the loving welcome of deceased friends and relatives and you have "paradise." With DBVs, is it any wonder that death loses its frightening grasp? What a delightful way to transition from this world to the next. As the author Elizabeth Barrett Browning said just before she died, "Beautiful."

Chapter 10

Bridging the Gap Between Life and the Afterlife

"Sister, you're trying to keep me alive as an old curiosity, but I'm done, I'm finished. I'm going to die."

Parting words of George Bernard Shaw

EXPERIENCE VS. SCIENCE

George Bernard Shaw was not afraid to die. His nurse may have had an issue with his upcoming departure, but Shaw was more than ready to move on. In society today, so many people are fearful of death. Science appears to perpetuate this fear with its linear view of the world. Western culture, along with its materialistic approach to science, has rendered the topic of an afterlife a dead issue. For most scientifically minded individuals, the thought is, "If it can't be measured, weighed, scientifically documented or reproduced in a lab, why bother?"

Why bother indeed! As you have seen, many people are seeing, hearing, feeling and sensing an afterlife existence. Aren't our claims worthy of investigation? According to most of the scientific community, the answer is a resounding "No!"

From the pulpit, orthodox religion is quick to tout the beauty of an afterlife but will then promptly dismiss other-worldly experiences that congregants share. Most clergy perceive encounters with deceased relatives, angels, beings of light and celestial visions as nonsense. After sharing my afterlife encounters with a clergyperson, the typical response rarely involves wide-eyed interest and amazement, or even empathy. Instead, I am often confronted with some inaccurate, scientifically based explanation. I find this maddening!

Raymond Moody has received a great deal of criticism from clergy for his research into the near-death experience (NDE). In order to gain perspective on such criticism, Raymond now refers to these particular clergy members as "Fund-a-Christians." In my opinion, this researcher has the right idea. As opposed to feeling shamed, discounted or angry about being ridiculed, just laughing is better. From a personal perspective, such an attitude makes the path of investigation much easier to travel.

From a societal point of view, what is disturbing about the reproach Dr. Moody has received from certain Christian clergy is that the Christian ministry is not alone. Agnostics, Jews, Muslims, atheists, Buddhists and members of various other spiritual pursuits have all reported experiencing near-death experiences, after-death communications, out-of-body experiences and deathbed visitations. Many rabbis also quickly dismiss such accounts, seeing them as old superstition or unintelligent "rubbish." Nonetheless, a huge movement within the Jewish community is questing for information on mysticism. How in good conscience can the clergy openly preach about the joy of "life ever after" while ignoring the experiences of those sitting in the pews? Must these congregants continue to quietly whisper about their encounters, away from the ears of their so-called spiritual teachers?

I will never forget the day I tried to share an unusual vision I had with a particular woman friend. At the time, I was very confused, shaken and in need of a great deal of reassurance. Instead of support, her response to my account was, "Do you suppose you should have your eyes checked for cataracts?" Needless to say, I never told her anything again! I must say, over the years there have been times when even I have felt like some nut case being examined under a microscope. In this respect, I know I am not alone. In *Life After Death,* one of Kenneth Ring's patients shared a similar frustration after a near-death experience:

I find people are very standoffish when you start talking about it. You know, they'll say, "Oh really?" and they'll kind of hesitate away from you. I mean, it happened with the doctors at the hospital after the incident did happen to me. . . . They wouldn't listen. For a while I really felt that I was a little crazy, because every time I did broach the subject somebody would change the subject, so I felt the topic probably shouldn't be discussed.

In "Doctor-Patient Relationships in Terminal Illnesses" by C. A. Garfield (1978), another dying patient is quoted as stating the following after openly discussing his experiences. Such words speak for many.

I'll be damned if I share my feelings about dying with someone who manages a two-minute U-turn at the foot of my bed.

This man had some strong emotions about his upcoming death. Sadly, he too felt he had to remain silent. What a sorrowful note on which to leave this life. DBVs have a powerful influence over the dying and they should be used in a positive, healing manner. As sociologist Ian Currie stated in *You Cannot Die* (1978), "The power of deathbed visions is eerie. We find this same, inexplicable intensity over and over again. Patients who are in pain, wretched and frightened, are suddenly transformed, glowing with exaltation, eager for death." Shouldn't these visions be used to heal both the living and the dying? Instead of ignoring DBVs, we should look at the many healing benefits they can provide.

The Gifts of DBVs

After deathbed visitations, positive mood shifts in the dying are often noted. Languishing in a coma, a sixteen-year-old American girl became clearly conscious just before the end. (This account was originally taken from *The Hour of Death* by Osis and Haraldsson.)

> *"I can't get up," she said . . . and opened her eyes. I raised her up a little bit and she said, "I see him, I see him. I am coming." She died immediately afterwards with a radiant face, exultant, elated.*

This DBV brought serenity and solace to the dying girl. If only clergy and science could appreciate and accept this fact.

Can a DBV even bring about a positive change in the *personality* of a person close to death? According to a vision one woman had, yes! The following DBV report is also taken from *The Hour of Death*. This patient, a woman in her late seventies, had a bad reputation with the nurses who took care of her. She was described by one nurse as a very mean person who was always nasty. I suspect this poor woman was scared to pieces of dying! Notice how a DBV positively impacted her disposition.

One night she called me to see how lovely and beautiful heaven is. Then she looked at me and seemed surprised. "Oh, but you can't see it, you aren't here (in heaven), you are over there." She became very peaceful and happy . . . and she permitted her meanness to die. . . . I don't think these are hallucinations, they are . . . very real.

The fear of sinking into death is prevalent in society today. Death and dying researcher Dr. Elisabeth Kübler-Ross has referred to America as a "death-denying culture." In our society, we have a tendency to sidestep the whole death issue as much as possible.

In certain cultures, preparation for the dying experience begins in one's forties. The thought is that if preparation begins early, people will be prepared when death "comes a-knocking." American culture treats death very differently, holding it at arm's length at all times. As a matter of fact, in one community I lived in, the denial of death was so strong there wasn't a funeral home to be found. Michael and I used to joke about how we were going to have to make it across the county line before dying! I hypothesize that those people who become more discontent as death approaches are actually terrified. Deathbed visions typically eliminate this fear for the dying.

Empathy

Sharing about deathbed visions with someone who is close to death is also very consoling. Though such a person may not have experienced a DBV, knowing that others have can reduce the fear of death. For the dying, such knowledge often bridges the gap between life and death.

A number of years ago, I went to California to appear on a television talk show hosted by Marilu Henner, who appeared on the TV sitcom *Taxi*. I was promoting a book, and her producer asked me to appear on the program as a marital expert. Before I said yes to my producer friend, I had one very special request. I needed to make a quick trip to Central California to visit my dying paternal grandmother. The producer graciously agreed to let me make this journey before the show was taped in Los Angeles.

My two young boys, Michael and I went to visit my grandmother in the raisin capital of the world, Fresno, California. As soon as I saw her, I knew death was near. Her once-beautiful, thick white hair had thinned, and she looked very tired. Knowing no one else in my extended family would talk to her about death and dying, I felt obligated to share with her what I knew about deathbed visions. When I started to tell her about death, she became absolutely petrified. Having always known she was terrified of dying, I had a great sense of sadness for her.

Having no fear of death myself, I was able to gently tell her what to expect at the moment of her passing. While I cautiously spelled out all I had learned over the years about the dying process, I noticed she began to calm down and really listen. I cried buckets of tears when I left her side, because I knew it would be the last time I would see her alive. In spite of my mourning, I was glad I had been able to offer her comfort. Several months after this, she quietly passed on. Thinking back on this time, I'm so grateful I was able to talk to her about death before it was too late. Sharing deathbed visions with frightened loved ones who are ending life is a powerful experience. When we do this, we lessen their anxiety and fear.

I have a cousin who was at one time also extremely uncomfortable with the topic of death. Several years after my grandmother passed over, my cousin called and asked if I would come with her to visit her dying mother. I happened to be back in my hometown that weekend visiting my grandfather, so I said, "Sure, no problem." Her mother was a chronic alcoholic and by the time she hit her sixth decade of life, her body was in horrible shape. My cousin said that the doctors had told her death was just around the corner.

We drove past the fragrant date, lemon and orange trees on the way to the nursing home where my cousin's mother was staying. When I saw her, my heart broke. Alcoholism had ravaged her small body. Though very frail, she asked us into her room and then with a flick of the remote control, she turned off her television. My cousin told her who I was and as we sorted out the family tree, I thought, "There but for the grace of God go I." Having heavily nipped at the sauce during my twenties, I quickly realized her fate would have been mine if I had not "put the plug in the jug."

After visiting for a while, my cousin and I loaded her mother up in a wheelchair and went for a stroll. Something told me I was going to have to bring up the topic of death soon. Before I could say a word, this little woman announced, "You don't know how rotten I feel about having drank myself into this mess. It's so embarrassing to be the family drunk!"

With this, I burst out laughing, and replied, "Honey, you aren't the only drunk in the family! Get in line! There are tons of us boozers in this clan."

Startled, she asked, "What on earth do you mean?"

Once again I chuckled and said, "I have been dry for a long, long while, but there was a time when I couldn't leave the stuff alone."

When she heard this, a huge smile crept across her face as she said, "You mean I'm not the only one?"

Taking a seat next to her I took her hand in mine and answered, "Hell no!" Having loosened things up a bit, I knew now was the time to talk about her upcoming death.

As I shared a few deathbed visions with her, she experienced a huge sense of relief. I could actually feel the weight of terror lifting off of her shoulders. Then I decided to tell her about the near-death research of Raymond Moody and

Kenneth Ring. I discussed with her the characteristics of an NDE. Her face began to light up. We talked about the tunnel she might see when she left her body at the point of death, and then said, "Don't be surprised if some long-lost dead relative meets you on the other side!" With this we laughed and talked about who that relative might be.

She continued to listen intently as I described deathbed visions of beautiful heavenly fields and multicolored landscapes. We also talked in depth about the bright loving light encountered by many of those who have had a near-death experience. Finally, I ended our conversation with, "There is absolutely nothing to be afraid of." With this she shed a few tears.

At that moment, I felt so blessed to have been in town before she passed. Talking with her about dying had brought her peace of mind. The healing it had provided for her gave me an indescribable feeling. When I left, I wished her a gentle death. She smiled and said, "I'm looking forward to that." Very shortly after this, my cousin called to say her mother had died while they were talking together on the phone.

Deathbed visions not only serve the experiencer, but others who are also close to making the big transition. Though my cousin grieved the physical loss of her mother, she too was comforted in knowing death was not the end.

In the following DBV account, a daughter-in-law lovingly

sorts out a vision her dying father-in-law has had. Once again we see how DBVs can be used as a tool of healing for both the living and the dying.

My father-in-law suddenly became ill last year. One day when visiting him, he asked me if I had seen the Grim Reaper out in the hall. Thinking he was joking (he always joked around), I laughed and said, "No."

When I got home, I suddenly had this powerful feeling that I needed to talk to him about what he said. Being a longtime, strong believer in angels, I knew I could do this. I went back the next day, but before going had asked God to give me a sign telling me to share with my father-in-law what was really in my heart. When I walked into his room, he told me he had a dream last night, and that in that dream, he talked to God. Upon hearing this, I knew it was my confirmation to speak.

I told him that the Grim Reaper was not in the hall. I told him that when his time came, an angel would come and that when he saw the angel, he should go with her. I told him not to be afraid, "The angel will take you to the light where you will be reunited with your wife and all of the friends and family that have gone before you."

He was in disbelief. He said he had done some things wrong and wasn't sure that this was going to happen to him. He was afraid. I told him God was a God of unconditional love, and that God knows we all do the best we can at the time we do things. . . . My father-in-law asked me how I knew these things and I told him he was just going to have to trust me on this one!

After our talk, I felt he was more at peace. He died about a week later. I was glad I was able to make his transition an easier one.

This woman gave a frightened dying man a real gift. Her support and reassurance allowed him to die peacefully. His dream of God and her conversation also made his passing easier. Family members can greatly assist loved ones as they leave. In the long run, avoiding talk about death never helps the one who is crossing over, nor those remaining on this side.

BOUNDARIES, PLEASE!

You might be asking yourself, "I have just learned that many people have heard their dying loved ones talk about such visions, and it was acknowledged that those at their bedside often get a quick look at the afterlife. With regard to my *own* experience, where do I go from here? Is it really wise for me to openly share? What is the game plan?"

In 1990 I wrote a book entitled *Learning to Say No: Establishing Healthy Boundaries.* In this book I discussed the importance of having healthy boundaries and taking care of ourselves in our relationships with other people. One aspect of a healthy boundary involves knowing "who" to share "what" with.

Many experiencers of the unseen world feel over-whelmed with emotion after their encounters. During such times, people are often engulfed by an incredible desire to share their knowledge with family, friends or whoever will listen. We want those around us to feel the joy we have tasted in recognizing that death isn't the end. Unfortunately, not everybody is ready to embrace what we know to be true.

After expressing to a very strict religious relative the beauty of my encounter with my mother, I was told I was following the path of Satan. My more scientifically minded friends just scoffed and said, "You are so eccentric, weird!" and then pulled back from me.

When I first began telling people about my interest in DBVs, their reactions always gave them away. Some people are very interested in the topic. They usually had little fear of death and they wanted to pick my brain about what I might know. Other folks feared death, but wanted to do something about this and were working toward developing a healthy philosophy. Finally, some individuals were seri-ously death-phobic. They rarely wanted to talk about it and were often very quick to change the subject if death was brought up in conversation.

After recognizing and sorting out these different reac-tions, I had to take several steps before I continued to share my experience, strength and hope with others. First, I had to learn to find folks who, like myself, had experienced DBVs and related phenomena. Talking with others who understood what I had been through was not only validating, but it made me feel "normal"! Second, after I began to feel secure about my experiences, the discounting remarks of family, friends and acquaintances carried less impact. In other words, I was able to reach a place where I didn't really care whether or not my DBV and ADC accounts were accepted by others. I knew they were real for me and respected the fact that those who had difficulty with my experiences were exactly where they needed to be on their spiritual journey. My job is not to convince all of humankind that my reality is true for everybody.

My message to you is: When you share your experience, choose people who will be accepting and excited about hearing what you have to say. We risk ridicule if we are not careful about our audience for relating these blessed events. If you look hard enough, you will find those doctors, clergy, friends and family members who are looking for individuals like you to talk to. A growing number of people from all walks of life want to know more about these experiences. Many experiencers are looking for someone to share with, and numerous people who have not had such encounters are desperate to hear about them.

To find such a person, use your boundaries. Test the waters. Don't jump in with both feet unless you know the water is safe! Comments like, "I had a bit of an unusual experience when Dad died," or "I wonder if anybody else has ever seen what I saw as Mom passed," are useful "feeling out" statements. When I first approached my rabbi about my contact with the afterlife, I was very subtle. Once I recognized he was interested, I slowly shared bits and pieces of my experiences with him. Eventually, he too felt safe enough to tell me about some of the unusual happenings he had encountered.

If the person you are talking to is not interested, they will let you know this very quickly with remarks like, "Yeah, death is strange. I try to avoid talking about it," or "The imagination and the dying brain can play a lot of tricks on you." If you hear something like this, know you are probably with an individual who is not able to hear about your experiences. Notice my emphasis of "able." They may be incapable of hearing you because of *their own* issues with death. When this happens, know that this is not about you. It is their issue, not yours.

If you discover that the person you are talking with has an interest in hearing about your otherworldly experience, proceed slowly. Start out by giving them just a fraction of your tale. For example, when talking about seeing his father in spirit form, my husband Michael always begins by saying, "I saw something incredible the day after my Pop passed. If I had not seen it myself, I don't know if I would have given credence to it." Then he waits for a reaction. If there is true interest, he will continue with a statement like, "You may not believe what I am about to tell you, but I must say, it was very real for me." As you build up to sharing the actual experience, you will be able to tell just how open your recipient is. By thinking before speaking about afterlife adventures, we are protecting ourselves with healthy boundaries. In this manner we go about finding others with whom we can safely share.

Once you feel comfortable with your experience, skepticism in the eyes of nonbelievers will not hurt you. Early on, when those around us respond with doubt to our brushes with the afterlife, we can find ourselves withdrawing, feeling as if we are alone in our experience. As time goes on, we may retreat even more. For years I didn't tell a soul about my experiences. Then, I became an open book, sharing everything with everybody. Eventually I grew tired of watching the eyebrows rise as I heard one more time that I was plagued with a "vivid imagination." I needed some time to develop a few boundaries for determining with whom sharing was appropriate.

Sympathetic Organizations and Other Outlets for Sharing

For those of you who are feeling that absolutely no safe place can be found to share what you've learned, several organizations can provide you with support and validation. The International Association for Near-Death Studies is an organization of scientists, scholars, near-death experiencers and interested members of the public, dedicated to understanding the human consciousness as it relates to the processes of both life and death. IANDS groups can be found across the country. In these groups, people come together to discuss deathbed visions, out-of-body experiences, after-death communications and near-death experiences. Within the safety of such environments, these topics can be discussed openly, intelligently and without ridicule. Feeling supported can make a world of difference, and the compassion found in these groups is wonderful. This organization is incorporated as a nonprofit group. To find an IANDS meeting near you, write to:

IANDS
P.O. Box 502
East Windsor Hill, CT 06028

Another organization is the American Society for Psychical Research, which has existed since 1885. DBV researcher Dr. Karl Osis was the director of research for this institution in 1962. The ASPR is the oldest psychic research organization in the United States. They have a wealth of information on unusual paranormal activity. Renowned Harvard psychologist William James was a card-carrying member of ASPR, and today countless researchers investigating unexplained phenomena have found support in this organization. To find out more about ASPR write to:

The American Society for Psychical Research
5 West 73rd Street
New York, New York 10023
or telephone:
(212) 799-5050

Cyberspace offers another rich source of immediate, hands-on access to information. Like any other area of investigation, experiences of deathbed visions, near-death experiences and after-death communications are openly discussed in chat rooms and on message boards on the Internet. Learning how to surf or navigate the Internet to find these resources involves a phone line, a willingness to learn and—these days—only basic computer skills. Once these goals are accomplished, connecting with others who have had afterlife experiences, or who are interested in such topics, is easy. If you already know how to access the Internet, plug the word "afterlife" into your search engine and explore. You can quickly contact other individuals who are eager to talk about deathbed visions and a host of related topics.

Refer also to the bibliography at the end of this book. Many of these publications can be found at your local library or at online booksellers. Most of the referenced work also contain bibliographies that will lead you to even more reading material. As one client recently said to me, "I had no idea there was so much written information on this stuff! The more I read, the more I learn there is an awful lot out there to be explored!"

You Can Be Your Own Medium

One of the consequences of the increased interest in life after death is the sudden proliferation of so-called mediums or psychics who profess to speak to our loved ones on the other side. Usually, they will only agree to engage in this activity for you after receiving a sizable amount of money. This particular issue causes me much distress. Some individuals in society are incredibly gifted at being able to communicate with the deceased. As I have journeyed the path of otherworldly exploration, I have come across a number of kind, honest, caring individuals who are very connected to the psychic ability all of us possess. The fees they charge cover their living expenses, and they aren't out to gouge the public. Sadly, a few rotten apples are present in every crowd, especially within the world of psychics and mediums.

A number of those who say they are "gifted" are no more psychic than you or I. As a matter of fact, you just might be more in touch with your "sixth sense" than the most advertised of psychics. Also, many of these so-called mediums can charge as much as two hundred to one thousand dollars per session. Personally, I find fees of this size offensive. Before you spend your hard-earned cash on a psychic, know that you can be your own medium in contacting your loved ones on the other side.

A Tale of Grief-Driven Stupidity

When a beloved relative of mine passed years ago, I was very upset not only about her death, but a number of family issues. On the recommendation of a friend, I contacted a certain self-professed medium. She gave me her fee schedule and though it was higher than my own clinical fee for psychological services, I was desperate, so I paid the requested "love donation." I made an appointment with this woman months in advance. She had told me her schedule was very booked and I ended up taking time away from my own office practice for this appointment. During our initial conversation, I was grieving, crying and incredibly upset, yet she would not take the time to offer me words of comfort. This behavior sent up a red flag for me, but unfortunately I ignored it.

Having been in the "shrink" business for many years, I know how desperate those in pain can be. Taking time to have compassion for such individuals is always extremely important. A little bit of understanding and a few kind words can go a long way. Hindsight is always 20/20, but at that time, in spite of my own clinical awareness, my grief ruled the day. I scheduled at her convenience, paid up-front and then waited with anticipation for the appointed time.

When that day arrived, I was where I was supposed to be, but she was nowhere to be found. Distressed and angry, I decided the session was not meant to be. The following day, I contacted her and told her I wanted my money back. She became extremely angry with me for not wanting to reschedule. When my money was returned, I noticed the check was not for the full amount I had originally sent. Inquiring about this, I was told she had deducted phone call expenses. Her deductions were much more than the cost of the phone call. Needless to say, I was ripped off!

My reason for sharing this embarrassing tale with you is twofold. First and foremost, if you are grieving the loss of a loved one, know this is an incredibly vulnerable time for you. Losing a beloved friend or family member can be a heart-wrenching experience. At such times, we are at risk for being preyed upon by less-than-honorable individuals. If you feel you need to speak with a professional medium, spend some time shopping around before you make a final decision. I have been investigating mediums for years and have enough tales of dishonesty to fill another chapter in this book. Interestingly, I have received more accurate information from psychics at carnivals than I have from high-dollar, Hollywood "psychic to the stars" mediums. An expensive fee schedule will not guarantee you an honest reading from a psychic or medium. So, be very careful.

Second, you can make contact with your loved ones on the other side yourself. It really isn't that hard. Try the following techniques and if they don't work the first time, be persistent. Try again!

Pay Attention to Dream Time

Before you go to sleep, make sure you have a paper and pen at your bedside so that you can document your dreams upon awakening. As you lay your head on your pillow, look at a picture of your deceased loved one. Then close your eyes and visualize yourself sitting with this person. Ask them to visit you in your dreams that night. Tell them you really want to spend some time with them. If you have a hard time visualizing them in your mind's eye, picture the photograph and speak to it. Then, drift off to dreamland. If you are still feeling unsure about this process, hopefully the following account will give you food for thought.

* * *

Nighttime brings sleep, and the sleep state allows for access into other realms of existence. In 1925 James Jr.

began having some very unusual dreams about his deceased father, James Sr. As taken from "Case of the Will of James L. Chiffon," *Proceedings of the Society for Psychical Research* (1928), we read the following sworn statement from James Jr.

> *He appeared at my bedside again, dressed as I had often seen him in life, wearing a black overcoat which I knew to be his own coat. This time my father's spirit spoke to me. He took hold of his overcoat this way and pulled it back and said, "You will find my will in my overcoat pocket," and then disappeared. The next morning I arose fully convinced that my father's spirit had visited me for the purpose of explaining some mistakes. I went to my mother's and sought for the overcoat but found that it was gone. Mother stated that she had given the overcoat to my brother John who lives in Yadkin County about twenty miles northwest of my home. . . . On the 6th of July . . . I went to my brother's home . . . and found the coat. On examination of the inside pocket I found that the lining had been sewn together. I immediately cut the stitches and found a little roll of paper tied with a string which was in my father's handwriting and contained the following words:*
> *"Read the 27th chapter of Genesis in my daddy's old Bible."*

At this point in the tale, a Mr. Thomas Blackwelder continues with his sworn statement.

We made a search for the Bible and after some time we found it in a bureau drawer in the second story of the house. We took out the Bible which was quite old and was in three different pieces. I took one of the three pieces out of the book and Mr. Chiffon took the other two pieces, but it happened that the piece I had contained the Book of Genesis. I turned the leaves until I came to the 27th chapter and there found two leaves folded inwards and there was paper writing folded in these two leaves which purported to be the last will of James L. Chiffon.

Here is what was contained in this document.

After reading the 27th Chapter of Genesis (which concerns how Jacob unfairly wrested his father's estate from his elder brother, Esau), I, James L. Chiffon, do make my last will and testament, and here it is. I want, after giving my body a decent burial, my little property to be equally divided between my four children, if they are living at my death, both personal and real estate divided equal; if not living, give share to their children. And if she is living, you must all take care of your mammy. Now this is my last will and testament. Witness my hand and seal.

The document was signed by the deceased and dated "This January 16, 1919." A number of people swore this was James L. Chain's signature. It appears as though James Sr. had some unfinished business and he came to his son, James Jr., for assistance.

* * *

We too can make contact with our loved ones on the other side through our dreams. When you wake up, write out your dreams. Do this for at least a week. Like James Chiffon Jr., hopefully you too will have a visitation from a loved one living in the afterlife.

Letter Writing

When I decided to deal with my grief about my mother's early death, I began journaling to her daily. I wrote her a letter every day, at the same time of day, for six months. In these letters, I expressed my sadness, anger and hurt. Along with this, I also shared with her my life. As time went on, I started to feel her presence. Today she gives me certain signs to let me know she is near. Usually these particular happenings take place during the rough turns in my life. A particular picture on my bedroom wall will move on her birthday, death anniversary and if I'm particularly upset by some life event. Since it is behind a door and nobody except my husband and I know about this, we are convinced this is my mother's otherworldly calling card.

Afterlife Visualization

I have a favorite afterlife visualization technique that I use to make contact with those who have recently crossed over. This visualization will also work with those loved ones who passed some time ago. Find a comfortable spot in your home where you will not be disturbed for about forty-five minutes. Make sure the television is off and the phone is unplugged. I try to do this meditation when my children are at school. Make sure the clothing you are wearing is loose fitting. Have a pen and paper next to you so that you can write about your experience after the visualization.

* * *

Close your eyes and take several deep breaths. As you breathe in, imagine a pure light enters your body and flows into every one of your cells. As you exhale, visualize the stress leaving your body. Give this stress a color. I like to visualize myself exhaling red tension from my body.

Once you begin to feel relaxed, see yourself in a field full of brilliant color. Greens mix with colorful flowers as a gentle breeze whispers through the field. The air is cool and crisp. In the middle of the field is a small hill. On top of this hill you will see a beautiful chapel. Notice there is a path leading up to the place of peace.

As you begin your journey up the hill, let your fingertips brush the grasses and flowers swaying in the breeze. Notice the sweet scent in the air and listen for the celestial sounds of soft music coming from the chapel.

When you reach the doorway, you will see a bright light

emanating from inside. Imagine yourself moving toward this light. Come closer and you will see your loved one standing in the middle of this brilliant light. Visualize yourself taking his or her hand. As you stand there, tell your loved one how much you miss them. Let them know they are in your thoughts daily. Say everything you want to say. Don't hold back. Share all of your feelings. If you are angry about their death, say so. Cry if you need to and express your grief.

Once you have done this, ask this person if they are happy on the other side. Then listen to what it is they have to share with you. After he or she has finished talking, imagine the two of you embracing each other. As you embrace, tell your loved one you would like a sign from them that they are okay. (I had asked my mother to move the picture in my bedroom.) See if they are willing to give you a sign.

After this gentle embrace, imagine backing away from your loved one. As you do, you will see the light around them intensify. Eventually this person will disappear into the light, and then the brilliance of this light will begin to fade away. Once this happens, imagine walking out of the chapel, into the sunlight and the field of flowers. Sit in the field and reflect on your visit with this loved one. When you are ready, open your eyes and write about your experience.

* * *

This visualization can be very powerful. If you need to ask for support from others, do so. Be kind to yourself and know that the feelings you experience during this visualization are not only normal, but necessary for your healing and spiritual growth.

A Talk

Here is another visualization that will help you reach across the divide between life and the afterlife. For this particular experience, you might want to find an item that once belonged to your deceased loved one: clothing, jewelry, a favorite book or any other item. Having this belonging with you as you visualize your loved one can be very useful. Sit in a chair at a table where you can write. Have a pad of paper and a pen in front of you. Be sure the television and radio have been turned off. Any distraction should be avoided at this time. If you smoke, no cigarettes during the duration of this activity. Also, avoid eating or drinking while you sit at the table.

* * *

Begin by writing out a list of questions you would like to ask your friend or relative in the otherworld. Choose one question to ask. After you have done this, pick up and hold in your hands your loved one's belonging. A photograph will also work. If you have nothing belonging to this person, write their name on a piece of paper and hold this in your hands.

As you feel the belonging or photograph, close your eyes. Then, visualize your loved one and ask your question. Don't try to think how they would respond. Listen with your inner senses for their answer. What is the first response that comes to your mind? Open your eyes and write this down, even if it doesn't make sense. Then look at your next question. Close your eyes and then repeat this process until you have asked all of your questions.

During such visualizations, the image in our mind will occasionally disappear. If this happens, don't become concerned, as this is normal. In many instances, the answers will come even if you are not able to visualize your loved one. Also, it is common for there to initially be no response. Some people have reported seeing other images, such as colors, animals, buildings or even other people instead of their loved one. Ask this image why it is here instead of the one you are trying to visualize. Listen for a response or reaction. Be sure to write your answers down on the paper in front of you.

Once you have asked all of your questions, go through each of your answers and ask yourself, "What does this response mean to me?" When I first did this exercise with my mother, all I would see were graves and coffins, often in black, white and gray. These images had several very special meanings to me. I was holding on to my mother, not releasing her to the light because my grief was so immense. I had unfinished business with her. Aside from this, I was extremely angry with God about her early death. After I acknowledged my grief and anger, I was able to give myself permission to feel these emotions. My communications with my mother dramatically improved after I had spent time feeling the emotions I had been avoiding.

You are the most qualified person to interpret the images you see during this visualization. If you are still confused, write an essay titled, "What This Image Means to Me." Put together a written story about this image. Just make one up. See if your story provides you with any more clues.

* * *

THE BRIDGE BETWEEN THIS WORLD AND THE NEXT

Souls descend to Earth much like explorers venturing into unfamiliar and difficult terrain. A soul inhabiting a body may be likened to a deep-sea diver who steps into a heavy suit for protection from atmospheric conditions on the ocean floor. Or the incarnating soul can be compared to a mountaineer equipping himself to climb a rock face at high altitude with crampons, goggles and an oxygen mask.

The soul's mission is always the same: to search for knowl-edge, to learn from experience and, in maturity, to help others do likewise. At the close of each exploration, it is the animating spirit within the bodily envelope that survives physical death. This is the "you" that cannot die.

These incredible words come from Ian Currie in *You Cannot Die* (1995). I too believe life is nothing more than a journey and that I am but "a spiritual being having a human experience." Every one of us is dealt a particular genetic deck of cards at birth. In my case, I inherited the genes for alcoholism, Crohn's disease, size-twelve feet and a six-foot-tall body. Because of my genes, my childhood was painful, and I struggled through early adulthood. If life were based only on my genetic makeup, I should have departed this life long ago.

Thankfully, during the life experience we are all offered many paths of travel. Each path takes us on a different journey, and the choice to follow a particular course is always ours. Our living experience does not have to be totally determined by our genes. Instead of continuing to drink, I quit. Because I changed my lifestyle and diet, the Crohn's disease has been in remission for years. I learned how to create clothing specifically for my tall, lean frame and sought out specialty stores that cater to women with big feet! As for my difficult childhood, I did what I needed to do to heal and make peace with my genetics.

Life is a journey with lessons to learn. When we are done with life, we move on, review what we have learned and prepare for the next challenge. Our deceased loved ones are doing just that. As a friend of the author Ian Currie said to her visiting father, thirteen years after his death, "My God, what are you doing here? Please go back to where you belong."

Our loved ones on the other side of the veil are moving toward the next adventure, with even more experiences to embrace. Those of us who have had a peek at their afterlife existence understand. We know our loved ones are right where they are supposed to be, and we understand their spiritual development continues. They have been reunited with friends and family who traveled before them. From reading the series of deathbed visions presented in this book, we can be assured of such reunions and look forward to them.

Before we end this chapter, I thought I would share with you the impact DBVs have had on surviving members in my own family. I know for myself, my experiences have erased for me any fear of death. Michael, my husband, who used to believe his father's "we become worm food and that's it" philosophy, refuses to debate this topic with non-believers. His comment is, "Why should I bother? I know what I saw and I feel no need to prove anything to anybody. It's a nonissue. When I croak, I know where I'm going."

Because my children have been able to openly ask questions about death, dying is now seen as a normal, routine life experience. They believe, "You go from here to some other place. And it's fun." Aaron is convinced the afterlife existence consists of pizza, soda, nonstop baseball games and his Da.

As a family, when we mourn the passing of a loved one, we understand that we are grieving the physical loss. We recognize that though our friend or family member no longer has "skin," the only thing death changes is communication possibilities. Contact might become more difficult, but we truly believe our loved ones still hear us. With this knowledge, each of us continues to talk to those we love on the other side in our own way. We do this because we all agree that relationships still exist after death.

Are we as a family alone in our beliefs about life after death? Read the following comments from people who have had DBV experiences in their own family and then decide.

This experience has been wonderfully reassuring. It allowed me a glimpse of my daughter in her new life with its new roles, and it also helped me to begin establishing a new relationship with her. It helped me believe that she could indeed hear me and that she was the caring person I remembered.

* * *

I no longer see death as an end. I have no fear of it, but see it as a part of life and living. Our loved ones are with us always, just not on this plane. Our loved ones on the other side will help guide us all our days.

* * *

I feel so blessed to have been able to witness my father-in-law's deathbed vision. From his facial expression, I could tell he was excited to see all of the people who were visiting him from the other side. I have no fear of death and know for certain that you will see your loved ones when you pass to the other side.

* * *

I saw my dying wife leave her body. Having a vision of her transition into the spirit realm has made it easier for me to never worry about her. I always know that she is with God and that her transition was easy. Also, my vision of her transition helps me to know, very deeply, that she continues to exist. . . . This has helped me stay open to the after-death communications that came in the following months. Also, I've always known, throughout my widowhood, that she is available to me for spiritual support.

* * *

My experience with my father showed me that in spite of all of his human faults, he has a pure and perfect spirit. I have total knowledge that the soul is eternal, and I have had personal experience with my father's total love for me. My father's soul is pure and perfect love. I have experienced how this physical world can be controlled by higher forces for coincidences (God-incidences) to happen.

* * *

It has brought me positive feelings about the afterlife.

* * *

I am not afraid to die now.

* * *

By having the experience with my mother-in-law's passing, I have come to terms with what I believe in as far as spirituality and an afterlife are concerned. This experience has taken me on a journey that I had not thought possible.

* * *

My father's dying experience has given me peace knowing that my dad has not really died, but merely moved on in his spiritual journey. I am grateful that he didn't go alone and was accompanied by an angel and was met by those who loved him. This is a source of great comfort to me.

* * *

Finally, here is what my oldest son Aaron said after his grandfather passed.

When playing baseball, I always ask Da to help me hit the ball. Every time I remember to do this, it works! I know he hears me.

If you have not yet caught a glimpse of the other side, grab on to the experiences of others. You can learn from them, and with this learning your own fear of the unknown will lessen.

We as a life-form, living on this planet—one within a cosmos grander than we can ever imagine—have a great deal more to learn about ourselves and our interconnectedness with the universe at large. Though our loved ones are not in the physical form we call life, they are still living and we are still connected to them. They are but a breath away.

Blessings to those of us who "trudge" the road toward spiritual enlightenment.

Afterword

I have thoroughly enjoyed doing this book. I have wanted to write it for many years. My hope is that these words have given you comfort, hope and something to contemplate. If you have had an unusual experience with the passing of a friend or loved one, I would enjoy hearing from you. I can be reached by e-mail at *carla.wills@brandon.net*, or you may write to me at:

Carla Wills-Brandon, Ph.D.
P.O. Box 2299
Galveston Island, Texas 77553-2299

 # Appendix

A Note to Medical Personnel, Mental-Health Professionals and the Clergy: How to Respond to Patients and Family Members Who Experience Deathbed Visitations

Just the other day, I was at my older son's tennis match. He was playing doubles with the Baptist preacher's son, Nathan. Aaron and Nathan soundly beat the other team, and the parents were delighted. After a round of "way to go" and hand shaking, the Baptist preacher looked at me and said, "I hear congratulations are in order. Didn't you just finish a couple of books?"

I replied, "Why, yes."

The preacher then said, "I'm really interested in your book on deathbed visions. In my line of work, I come across this phenomenon all of the time. Funny thing is, although it's a common occurrence, nobody seems to want to talk about this. Especially my peers."

His lovely wife then added, "Why is that? Are people afraid of being judged? Is this why so few people will discuss such things?"

"Yes," I replied. "I think you have just hit the nail on the head."

Both Rabbi Kessler—who wrote the foreword of this book—and this particular preacher—the spiritual leader of one of the local Baptist churches near my home— understand the importance of listening to and validating the deathbed visitations their congregants share with them. Unfortunately, among most clergy, such open-mindedness is not the norm.

Luckily for me, I have also been blessed to have friendships with medical practitioners who know how to respond to DBV reports.

"It's extremely important to take the time to listen to patients, especially when they are sharing strong spiritual experiences such as deathbed visions or near-death experiences," was a comment I received from Dr. Mitchell Wilson, a popular internist at the University of Texas Medical Branch.

Another friend of mine, Dr. Clayton Moliver, added, "These visions can provide a great deal of comfort to patients and their family members and should never be discounted or ignored by medical personnel." Like my clergy friends, my medical buddies are in the minority in their viewpoint on DBVs and other spiritual experiences.

When confronted with an otherworldly report, medical people and clergy aren't the only ones who need to spend more time "listening." In my business as a mental-health caregiver, I have come across numerous people in my own profession who regularly dismiss, negate and ignore accounts of after-death communication (ADC), out-of-body experiences (OBEs), deathbed visions (DBVs) and other spiritual adventures. When confronted with near-death experiences (NDEs), many of these mental-health professionals dive into long dissertations about how such visions are hallucinations, the by-product of an overactive imagination or stress. Upon hearing one of these types of accounts, some psychiatrists will commonly write out prescriptions for strong psychotropic drugs. Thankfully, a few of my peers understand the importance of these events.

One therapist friend of mine, Goldie Rappaport, CSW-ACP, LPC, believes these encounters can be spiritually healing. Recently, she shared with me an NDE that a physician friend of hers had experienced. Another psychologist acquaintance said he incorporated such visions into patient treatment plans and used them as a positive tool for self-discovery. A friend of mine who is a professor of psychology, Dr. Alex Seigel, told me, "The history of psychology is loaded with examples of spiritual investigation.

All one has to do to get a flavor of this is to pick up a work by William James. His writings are full of examples of spirituality as it relates to human consciousness. Most of James's comments on spirituality came after 1896–97 (his 'Lowell Lectures' on Exceptional Mental States), and are at the core of his 1902 book, *The Varieties of Religious Experience*." William James is often viewed as the father of psychology. His works are required reading for psychology students.

I agree with Dr. Seigel that among the sciences, psychology has since its inception had an interest in spiritual matters. Carl Jung not only had an NDE, but was convinced that spiritual matters greatly affected our psychological makeup and thus should be explored further. Sadly, too few mental-health practitioners help their patients take this journey.

Providing emotional support to a DBV, NDE, ADC or OBE experiencer really isn't that hard. The key element involves the ability to listen to the account and be supportive of the experience. Whether you believe in such phenomena or not, your duty—as a human-service provider for those in your care—is to support, not negate, such experiences. Certain comments, as follows, should definitely be avoided:

1. "I believe these experiences are just fabrications of the mind."

2. "I recently read research which suggests that these experiences are only the by-product of a dying brain."
3. "I really think your dying relative or friend was only hallucinating. S/he wasn't really seeing anything."
4. "You have been under tremendous stress, and I really do feel your mind has begun to play tricks on you."
5. "You (your friend/your relative) didn't actually see, hear or feel that. You are making too much out of this, and I don't believe this is good for you."
6. "Our church doesn't acknowledge such things."
7. "These visions are not of God. They are evil."
8. "You are in grief over your loss (or fearful of death). During these trying times, we all want to believe in such things. I suspect this is just wishful thinking."

The above remarks are based on personal experiences, religious belief systems and life philosophy. They reflect biased opinions. Although they may be true for a particular health-caregiver, they can quickly negate any healing potential that the ADC, NDE, OBE or DBV may possess for an experiencer. In most instances, such remarks are damaging. Silence accompanied by a compassionate nod of the head would be more healing.

As a health-care worker you should understand that projecting your personal spiritual reality onto those who trust you with their care is always inappropriate. Nor should you ever try to persuade a client or patient into believing that their spiritual experiences are not real. To the person who has experienced such phenomena, the encounters are typically "very real" indeed.

A useful approach to a patient who presents such spiritual encounters as we are discussing here is to ask open-ended questions. When confronted with a DBV or other related experience, health-care providers and clergy can use the following open-ended questions to prompt patients, congregants or clients to offer additional information and to search for insight into how the experience has affected them.

1. "How has this experience bettered your life? What feelings are you having about this?"
2. "What comfort did the vision or experience provide for you?"
3. "Have you learned anything from this experience?"
4. "How has this experience improved your view of you, the world around you and your spirituality?"
5. "What can you take from this experience and apply to improve the quality of your life?"

Open-ended questions can help experiencers in your care positively integrate the reported spiritual account into current life situations. Potential positive outcomes include reducing feelings of grief as well as the fear of impending death. In other words, even if you believe that for you personally such accounts are "not real," you can still use reported DBVs, ADCs, OBEs and NDEs to improve the quality of care and emotional support for the people you see.

Experiencers are often just reaching out for validation of their otherworldly encounters. Such a request, however, can create a sense of uneasiness for clergy and health-care workers. After hearing accounts of this nature, if asked, "Do you believe me?" possible response include:

1. "Yes, I believe you! What a powerful experience. Tell me more."

2. "Gee, can I ever relate!" (If you have had such an experience or know of others who have encountered similar phenomena, it is perfectly acceptable to disclose this.)

3. "It's not important whether or not I believe you. This is your experience. Tell me what it has done for you."

4. "I don't know what to tell you. This is incredible. Let me ask around to see if I can find any books or resources that might help you better understand your experience." (A few of these resources can be found in this book's bibliography.)

5. "It sounds like you have had an exciting, life-transforming event. You might need to spend some time processing this. Though I'm not real familiar with such things, I would be more than happy to hook you up with someone who is. Are you interested?" (Hospices, The International Association of Near-Death Studies

and The American Society for Psychical Research are just a few of the organizations you can contact to find support for your congregant, client or patient.)

Actively listening and not negating these experiences is the key to providing those in your care with the emotional support they need. Such an approach is complicated only when you attempt to force your own personal beliefs onto the situation, which disrespects the integrity of the person you are there to assist.

Among the sources of counterproductive behavior on the part of health-care providers and clergy are personal issues with death, dying, spirituality, organized religion and unresolved family-of-origin history. The unresolved death of a loved one can block the ability to provide supportive responses to people who are grieving. If you have concerns, fears or lingering difficulties with any of the above, I strongly suggest you seek out assistance from a qualified therapist, spiritual advisor or mentor. Once your personal emotional house is in order, you will be better prepared to objectively serve and support people who come to you for care.

Those of us in the human services industry have a powerful role to fill. People in need seek us out and look to us for support. The greatest gift we can provide for the dying and those who grieve them is a bit of our time and our empathy. Such a small gift can provide a world of healing.

Bibliography

Aries, Philippe, *The Hour of Our Death*, trans., Helen Weaver. London: Allen Lane, 1981.

———. *Images of Man and Death*, trans., Janet Lloyde. Cambridge, Mass.: Harvard University Press, 1985.

Barrett, Sir William. *Death-Bed Visions: The Psychical Experiences of the Dying*. London: Psychic Press, 1926. Reprint. Northamptonshire, England: The Aquarian Press, 1986.

Bronsted, Johannes. *Vikings*. Trans. Estrid Bannister-Good. New York: Harmondsworth, Penguin, 1960.

Browning, Robert. "The Guardian Angel," from *Poetical Works of Robert Browning* (Cambridge Edition). Boston: Houghton Mifflin, 1974. (Originally published in *Bells and Pomegranates*, 1842).

Callanan, Maggie and Patricia Kelley. *Final Gifts*. New York: Bantam Books, 1997.

"Case of the Will of James L. Chaffin," *Proceedings of the Society for Psychical Research* 36 (1928): 517–24.

Currie, Ian. *You Cannot Die*. Great Britain: Element Books Limited, 1995.

Evans-Wentz, W.Y., ed. *The Tibetan Book of the Dead*. Oxford, England: Oxford University Press, 1960.

Faulkner, R.O., ed. *The Ancient Egyptian Book of the Dead,* rev. ed. London: British Museum, 1985.

Flammarion, Camille. *Death and Its Mystery at the Moment of Death.* New York: The Century Co., 1922.

Frematle, Francesca and Trungpa Chogyam. *The Tibetan Book of the Dead.* Boston: Shambhala Publications, 1975.

Gallup, George Jr. (with William Proctor). *Adventures in Immortality: A Look Beyond the Threshold of Death.* London: Souvenir, 1983.

Garfield, C.A. "Elements of Psychosocial Ontology: Doctor-Patient Relationships in Terminal Illnesses," in *Psychosocial Care of the Dying Patient.* New York: McGraw-Hill, 1978.

Guggenheim, William and Judy. *Hello from Heaven.* New York: Bantam Books, 1997.

Harpur, Tom. *Life After Death.* Toronto: McClelland and Stewart Inc., 1991.

Hyslop, James H. *Psychical Research and the Resurrection.* Boston: Small, Maynard and Co., 1908.

Kübler-Ross, Elisabeth. *On Death and Dying.* New York: MacMillan, 1969.

Miller, R. DeWitt. *You DO Take It With You.* New York: Citadel Press, 1955.

Moody, Raymond. *Life After Life.* Covington, Ga.: Mockingbird Books, 1975.

Morse, Melvin. *Transformed by the Light: The Powerful Effect of Near-Death Experiences on People's Lives.* New York: Villard Books, 1992.

Morse, Melvin (with Paul Perry). *Closer to the Light: Learning from the Near-Death Experiences of Children.* New York: Bantam Books, 1993.

Neiman, Carol and Emily Goldman. *Afterlife: The Complete Guide to Life After Death.* New York: Viking Penguin, 1994.

Oates, Stephen B. *Abraham Lincoln: The Man Behind the Myths.* New York: Harperperennial Library, 1994.

Osis, Karlis. *Deathbed Observations by Physicians and Nurses.* New York: New York Parapsychology Foundation, 1961.

Osis, Karlis and Erlendur Haraldsson. *At the Hour of Death.* New York: Avon Books, 1977.

————. "Deathbed Observations by Physicians and Nurses: A Cross-Cultural Survey," *The Journal of the American Society for Psychical Research* 71.3 (July 1977): 237–259.

Phantom Encounters: Mysteries of the Unknown. Alexandria, Va.: Time-Life Books, 1988.

"Proceedings of the Society for Psychical Research," 291, from *Annals des Sciences Psychiques.* (1899). Reprinted in *Death and Its Mystery at the Moment of Death.* By Camille Flammarion. New York: The Century Co., 1922.

Randles, Jenny and Peter Hough. *The After Life.* New York: Berkley Books, 1994.

Raphael, Simcha Paull. *Jewish Views of the Afterlife.* Northvale, N.J.: Jason Aronson, 1996.

Ring, Kenneth. *Heading Toward Omega: In Search of the Meaning of the Near-Death Experience.* New York: William Morrow, 1984.

————. *Life at Death: A Scientific Investigation of the Near-Death Experience.* New York: Coward, McCann and Geoghegan, 1980.

Ripley, Alexandra. *A Love Divine.* New York: Warner, 1997.

Romer, John. *Ancient Lives: The Story of the Pharaohs' Tombmakers.* London: Welderfeld and Nicolson, 1984.

Rose, Ronald. *Living Magic: The Realities Underlying the Psychical Practices and Beliefs of Australian Aborigines.* London: Chatto and Windus, 1957.

Smith, Susy. *Life Is Forever.* New York: Dell Publishing, 1974.

Snell, Joy. *The Ministry of Angels*. London: G. Bell and Sons, Ltd., 1918.

Solecki, Ralph S. "Shanidar IV: A Neanderthal Flower Burial in Northern Iraq." Science 190.28 (November 1975): 881.

"The Sunset of Bon Echo," from the abridged account given to the ASPK by Flora McDonald Denison. *Journal of the American Society for Psychical Research* 15 (1921): 114–23.

Swift, Jonathan. "Thoughts on Religion," from *Portable Swift*. New York: Viking Penguin Press, 1977.

Watson, Ian. "The Death of the Duke of Windsor," *Sunday Telegraph*, 30 November 1986: 8.

White, John. *A Practical Guide to Death and Dying*, 2d ed. Wheaton, Ill.: Quest Books, 1988.

Whitman, Walt. "Osceola," from *Leaves of Grass*. 1891–92. Reprinted New York: NAL-Dutton, 1954.

Wills-Brandon, Carla. *Learning to Say No: Establishing Healthy Boundaries*. Deerfield Beach, Fla.: Health Communications, Inc., 1990.

Wilson, Ian. *The After-Death Experience*. New York: Quill Publishing, 1987.